Software Engineering

A Practical Approach

Software Engineering

A Practical Approach

Laxmidhar V. Gaopande

Copyright

Dedication

This book is dedicated to all my colleagues and my team members of various companies where I have worked till date, my parents and my family members who always supported me and who inspired me to write this book. All those colleagues who supported me in carrying out my software engineering research and appreciated my research in software engineering area while executing various assignments for global customers which involved software projects and product engineering work across different technologies and platforms.

Summary of Contents

Table of Contents

Preface

I have executed many software projects and engineering assignments in India and abroad and I have carried out various software engineering researches while doing this work in terms of software development, metrix collection, estimations, project management etc. Lot of this work has been highly appreciated by my managers and my colleagues in various offices and end customers from all over the world. Their appreciation has motivated me to write this book.

I have spent 30+ years in software development and very well conversed with software projects and products of small, medium, large sizes, across different technologies and platforms along with traditional waterfall models to agile development, on site, offshore, dual shore and global delivery models of execution. I thought of sharing my experience with students at undergraduate, graduate level, teachers and practitioners from IT industry.

I have delivered many lectures in software engineering area and also published many papers in national and international conferences.

Readers will see very practical aspects of software engineering in this book and will get immensely benefitted by my experience in this field.

I sincerely feel this book will be very useful and will give good insights in software engineering practice.

Mumbai, India, 2020   Laxmidhar V. Gaopande

Acknowledgements

I like to acknowledge all my colleagues and team members who worked with me in various companies and were part of software development team while executing various software projects and product engineering work for global customers.

I like to acknowledge all those people who helped me to carry out various software engineering experiments and research on various software assignments.

I also like to acknowledge my parents and all my family members who were quite patient and tolerant while I was working on completing this book.

Author Biography

Author, Laxmidhar V. Gaopande has studied Bachelor of Engineering at VNIT Nagpur, Management Diploma at Symbiosis Institute of Business Management, Pune and Master of Technology at Indian Institute of Technology (IIT) Madras.

He is in software development area for more than 30+ years and has delivered more than 100+ software projects and products for global Fortune 500 companies from USA, UK, Germany, Israel, India etc. He has worked with Indian MNCs and in USA and UK as a Software Consultant. He has travelled immensely to many countries like USA, UK, Germany, Japan, Singapore, Israel, Italy, South Korea, Netherland, Switzerland, Norway and France till date and has interacted with various companies while doing various software assignments for them.

He has published many papers in software engineering in many national and international conferences and has delivered lectures on various subjects in many educational institutes and conferences in India and abroad. He has also filed many patents in USA.

His was also invited as visiting faculty to teach global MBA students subject of information technology and software engineering by a highly reputed MBA school in Dubai.

He is recipient of many prestigious awards and scholarships in his academic excellence.

Introduction

This book is meant for all kinds of software development professionals, software developers, students, teachers, managers or top executives to understand how important is software engineering in order to develop and deliver in time with high quality keeping in mind what a client needs.

The book is written based on rich experience the author has while dealing with global customers from countries like USA, UK, Germany, Israel, Italy and India. It covers 30+ years of author's rich experience in software development and product engineering while dealing with execution of projects and products for global customers.

The book tries to bring all important aspects of software engineering, important areas like software projects types, various delivery models, software development life cycle, quality systems, software requirements, analysis , design and architecture models, usability engineering, user experience, configuration management, release management, risk management, project management, estimation techniques, why projects fail, software support, case studies, exercises and useful data which author has used himself and found extremely useful while dealing with live projects in actual development and execution.

The various case studies are covered with intention of sharing learnings from each project and how that project would have been successful or would have caused little pain that it did actually. The case studies may serve as useful feedback to the readers.

The eighteen exercises at the end of book cover all the topics in this book with assignment of developing a new software system to make the understanding of all the concepts more clear.

Chapter 1

Overview

The mankind has always seen many evolutions. In case of computers we have seen many generations of computers, in case of software development we have seen many techniques and models of development evolving over the last few years and continue to evolve as technology matures, we have seen different coding languages getting developed and used by developers in different environment, platforms etc. as per the need and rolling out various projects.

Software engineering is a science. It has its own principles to follow in order to make software development a great success. Nothing happens in an adhoc manner, one has to keep on looking at best approaches in every task we do in order to ensure quality. Software engineering is not just a science but it is innovative, scientific, evolving and creative.

Software engineering is the science and art of engineering approach to software development. It involves specifying the requirements of software to be developed, designing, implementing and delivering within various constraints of cost, resources, infrastructure and timelines to meet the functional and non-functional requirements specified to meet the expectations.

The importance of software engineering is not felt immediately to many professionals as they begin their software career as programmers where everyone thinks deep expertise in a given coding language is a key to success. As one matures in his/her software development experience, one realizes that expertise of a language contributes 10 to 20% of overall project success, what are those other areas which impacts 80 to 90% of a project?, they are quality of specification, quality of design, quality of architecture, quality of code, quality of test plan, quality of testing, quality of documentation, quality of reviews, quality of project management etc.

One has to realize as early as possible in his/her software engineering career that one needs to develop mastery gradually in other areas mentioned above in order to execute a quality project to the satisfaction of customer who finally pays for the deliverables.

Experience is an important factor in any software project, a team which is experienced both in terms of domain knowledge and software engineering will be a winner any day. We see people migrating in their roles as they progress in their software career starting from Programmer, Analyst, Designer, Architects, Module Leader, Team Leader, Project Leader, Project Manager to VP – Engineering. I always found a gradual progression is better as one takes a deep experience at each stage. There is no substitute for experience in software engineering. A good programmer can be a good analyst; a good analyst can be a good designer and so on.

Some people believes that one need not go through all the stages mentioned above but can still be a good software engineer and can play role much bigger, however I tend to defer, it's true that we play more than one role at a time e.g. a person may be a designer, architect and technical leader.

It's important that a software engineering adherence is followed in order to deliver quality. Any short cuts or adhoc approaches will cause fatal impact in a given task or assignment which will be difficult to salvage as it might have caused enough irrevocable damages to the project under consideration.

In absence of software engineering I learnt that people will end up making overpromises in many parameters like cost, efforts, calendar time, quality etc. A good transparent approach to any development is a key to success. It is extremely important that all stakeholders are addressed in order to give optimum output and quality.

Is Software engineering an art or science?

Chapter 2

Software Development Projects and Stages

There are different types of projects in software development area and they need to be executed differently in terms of delivery model, development models and approaches and they go thru different stages and phases. The software development life cycle (SDLC) followed also varies.

2.1 Types of Software Projects and their Execution

The software projects can be fresh development type or enhancements and/or maintenance of existing projects and/or products. They can be executed in any of the following manner,

1. Fully Onsite
2. Fully Offshore
3. Dual Shore
4. Mix of Onsite and Offshore (initial and final stages onsite, rest offshore)/Global delivery model

The projects might be on **Fixed Cost Fixed Schedule** or **Time and Material** (T&M) Basis.

The various processes recommended are,

1. Feasibility Study
2. Risk Analysis
3. Requirement Specifications
4. Analysis, Architecture and Design (GUI design and Detail Design)
5. Coding and Unit Testing
6. Integration Testing
7. System Testing
8. Project Management
9. Configuration Management
10. Risk Management
11. Release management
12. Acceptance Testing
13. Documentation
14. Training
15. Post Acceptance Support

While doing the above, following activities take place,

1. Requirement Management
2. Configuration Management
3. Release Management
4. Project Management
5. Quality Engineering (Quality Control and Quality Assurance)
6. Status Reporting to Clients
7. Change Management
8. Internal Project Reviews on regular basis
9. Risk Identification, Mitigation and Risk Management
10. Metrics collection

During different stages of Software Development Life Cycle (SDLC) different work products (artefacts) are generated, each work product gets subjected to reviews to ensure quality.

Reviews can be of following types,

1. Walkthrough

2. Inspection

3. Peer Reviews

4. Supervisor Reviews

Traceability from one stage to another throughout the SDLC need to be ensured i.e. Requirements need to be mapped to Design, Design to Code, Code to Tests, Documents etc. so that there will be one to one correspondence between preceding, current and succeeding work products to ensure that no gaps exit and/or carried forward during the development to meet the full scope of project.

2.2 SDLC Stages

The various stages of software development life cycle (SDLC) are as follows:

Figure 2.1 SDLC Stages

1. **Feasibility Study:** The initial study to ensure that the project/product development is feasible in terms of technology, skills, hardware, schedule, performance expectation, cost etc.

2. **Risk Analysis:** Evaluation of all kinds of risk elements upfront and also to be shared with

customer to bring transparency in development. Risk mitigation plan also should be created.

3. **Project Initiation:** This is a stage of embarking on a project and there are few things Project Manager must define, outline in order to keep control on the project. The various things need to be set out are Functional definition, Contract, Quality Plan, Documentation Plan, Configuration Management Plan, Initial Design, Test Strategy and Test Plan, Acceptance criteria, Method of working on a project and Project Plan etc.

4. **Requirement Specifications:** Detail requirements, which are captured, either on the basis of client document and/or discussion, documented or sent for client review to ensure no gaps exist between client expectations and development team. This must be signed off as basis to undertake development.

5. **Analysis, Architecture and Design (GUI design and Detail Design):** Formal Analysis and Design, either SSADM (Structured System Analysis & Design Method) or OOA/OOD (Object Oriented Analysis/Object Oriented Design) or Service Oriented Design or Test Driven Development carried out before coding begins. The techniques like Unified Modelling Language (UML), UML diagrams etc. to be created with suitable tools.

6. **Coding and Unit Testing:** Disciplined approach to coding using well defined Coding Standards either given by client or defined by company to be strictly

adhered to ensure that code is uniform, readable, portable and maintainable across the teams and organization.

7. **Integration Testing:** Different Modules/Subsystems need to be integrated with proper Integration Plan and subsequent testing to ensure that interfaces and data transfers across modules are happening correctly.

8. **System Testing:** Detail System Testing with well-defined Test Plans to cover all live scenarios to which system to be subjected, test cases to be generated, test data to be created, customer supplied data to be used if available, White box testing, Black Box testing, Volume Testing, Stress Testing etc. to be carried out, as per the type of project and relevancy.

9. **Release Management:** Software projects and/or products go through proper release management cycles, for each release, proper release documentation, what is new in the release, known bugs, operating systems supported, and third party libraries if any required, open sources and their versions etc. need to be specified.

10. **Acceptance Testing:** This is final user acceptance testing either carried out at company if the setup similar to client site is created or the tests can be carried out at client site to get formal acceptance.

11. **Documentation:** Documentation should follow proper standards to create system manuals, installation manuals, user manuals, online help etc.

12. **Training**: Proper training is often required as a handover of new release to customers so that they can understand various new features, workarounds in case of some known bugs to make optimum use of delivered software.

13. **Post Acceptance Support:** Post Acceptance Support in the form of some days of warranty support where any defects detected in the software to be fixed at no cost. These defects are related to agreed specifications.

2.3 Software Engineering Steps in SDLC

The various software engineering steps in SDLC are as follows:

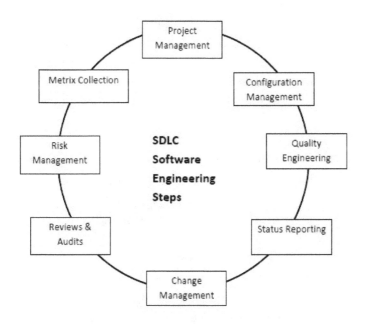

Figure 2.2 Software Engineering Steps in SDLC

1. **Configuration Management:** All configurable items either data, documents, sources to be configured. Usage of tools like Visual Source Safe, ClearCase, and SCCS can be made use of for version control and management.

2. **Project Management:** Project monitoring, Project control, Task Breakdown (TBD), Resource

deployment, Proactive risk identification to be carried out by Project Manager. Tools like MS-Project or other suitable tool can be used for tracking.

3. **Quality Engineering, Quality Control and Quality Assurance:** Quality engineering covers both QA and QC aspects. QC and QA can help to ensure that testing is proper, sample testing or 100% testing will be applied. Use of tools like MS-Test, WinRunner etc. can be used. Appropriate checklist will be prepared so that proper verification is carried out and often-detected bugs can be eliminated.

4. **Status Reporting to Clients:** Periodic status reporting, conference calls will be carried out to keep customer informed about the status of project or risks identified on ongoing basis to avoid any last minute surprises in terms of schedule.

5. **Change Management:** The ongoing additions and/or enhancements to already frozen specifications to be managed by proper Change management process so that impact of such change requests on schedule and cost can be carried out and the same to be communicated to client before changes are incorporated.

6. **Internal Project Reviews and Audits on regular basis:** Management reviews apart from Project Manager's review can be carried out to keep clear transparency in project progress. Internal audits to be carried out to ensure that proper practices are followed, if not the summary report of such reviews

and audits can alarm the development team to avoid future mistakes.

7. **Risk Identification, Mitigation and Risk Management:** Risk identification, mitigation and its management is essential part of any project and identified risks to be kept in control and client to be kept informed about such risks on regular basis.

8. **Metrics Collection:** Metrics collection to be done on regular basis to collect time spent on different activities, defect density, Lines of code (LOC)/Source Lines of code (SLOC) per person per month, Size of projects in terms of Function Points and/or Classes and their complexity details and in case of agile development user stores, velocity charts and burndown charts analysis outcome etc. to be collected. This can be very useful in future estimations.

2.4 Enhancements/Maintenance Projects

Such projects involve the following phases,

1. Study Phase
2. Configuration Management
3. Release Planning
4. Testing
5. Release
6. Documentation
7. Training
8. Post Release Support

1. **Study Phase:** In case of such project the existing software can be studied, all relevant documents like Requirement Specifications, Analysis, Design documents, User Manuals etc., Source code can be studied to get insight about the system to be enhanced or maintained.

2. **Configuration Management:** Proper Configuration Management of all configurable items like documents, test data, sources can be done.

3. **Release Planning:** Each new release to be planned in terms of new enhancements to be done and/or defects to be closed and release plan can be made. Each release to be led by a Program Manager or Product Manager.

4. **Testing:** Each release to be tested so that no regressions are detected. If there are any Automatic Test Suites exist or Test scripts exist, they can be used to subject each release to proper testing.

5. **Release:** Each release to end with list of proper checks of final release source code, list of known bugs, environment for the system to be deployed, should also form the part of release document.

6. **Documentation:** Proper documentation to be given to the customer, internal documentation with proper standards to be created so that maintenance becomes easy. Other documents like user manual, system manuals, installation manual etc. to be delivered.

7. **Training:** Proper training to the customer to make optimum use of software to be undertaken, computer based training aids can be generated if decided in contract.

8. **Post Release Support**: Defects detected after release to be added in defect database and the same will be tracked and taken to closure.

2.5 Tools Usage

Following tools can be used; there are many   other tools available and can be looked at as per the availability and budget.

1. MS – Project for Project Scheduling and Tracking
2. Visual Source Safe (VSS), ClearCase, SCCS for Configuration Management
3. MS-Test, WinRunner for Testing
4. Rational Rose for Analysis and Design representation
5. MS-Word for all documents
6. Defect Tracker System for logging defects and tracking

2.6 Templates for Work Products Described above

1. **Feasibility Study**

List of Requirements	Feasibility
1...	
2...	
3...	
4...	
5...	
Overall Feasibility	Yes/ No

2. **Risk Analysis**

List of Risks	Measure of Risks on scale of 1 to 10
1...	
2...	
3...	
4...	
5...	
Overall Risk	Low/Medium/High

3. **Requirement Specifications**

1.	Introduction
2.	Overview
3.	Top level system description
4.	List of Requirements
5.	Input, Output, Logical processing for each requirement

6.	Future plans
7.	Sample Data
8.	Sample Reports

4. Analysis and Design

1.	Introduction
2.	Overview
3.	Top level system architecture
4.	GUI
5.	List of Modules, Sub Modules, Subsystems, Class Hierarchy, Data Attributes, Member Functions, Services
6.	Class Details
7.	Pseudocode for methods

5. Coding Standards

1.	Introduction
2.	Overview
3.	List of data types and their naming convention
4.	Methods naming convention
5.	Style of comments
6.	History of creation
7.	Modification history

6. Unit Test Plan

1. Introduction
2. Overview of unit
3. List of test cases
4. Each Test case Input, Expected Results, Actual results

7. Integration Test Plan

1. Introduction
2. Overview of integration
3. List of integration issues to be monitored
4. List of integration tests
5. Each Test case Input, Expected Results, Actual results

8. System Test Plan

1. Introduction
2. Overview of system testing
3. List of system test cases
4. Each Test case Input, Expected Results, Actual results

9. Configuration Management Plan

1. Introduction
2. Overview of configuration plan designed
3. List of configurable items
4. How and when each item becomes configurable
5. List of control copy holders

10. Change Management Plan

1. Introduction
2. Overview of change management
3. Change request
4. Analysis of change request
5. Impact of change request on cost and schedule
6. OK to proceed: Yes/ No

11. Project Plan

1. Introduction
2. Overview
3. Development methodology
4. Resource plan
5. Software required
6. Hardware required
7. Training needs
8. Quality plan
9. Metrics plan
10. Exit criteria

12. Project Management

1.	List Of milestones
2.	Schedule
3.	Resource allocation
4.	Risk management
5.	Slippages
6.	Contingency planning

13. Status Reporting

1.	Status for the duration
2.	Prepared By
3.	Activities planned
4.	Activities completed
5.	Activities not completed, reason for not completed
6.	Activities planned for the next duration
7.	Risks

14. Release Plan

1.	List of activities for release
2.	Prepared By
3.	Enhancements
4.	Additions
5.	Defects planned for closure
6.	OS and platforms to be supported
7.	Alpha release to be completed by which date
8.	Beta release to be completed by which date
9.	Final release date

15. Release Notes

1.	Release details
2.	Prepared By
3.	Enhancements
4.	Additions
5.	Defects closed
6.	OS and platforms supported
7.	Known defects and workaround

16. Metrics Details

1.	Metrics details
2.	Prepared By
3.	Size of software
4.	FPs/ Number of Classes, methods, services, user stories, velocity as per the development methodology
5.	LOC/SLOC
6.	Defect Density observed
7.	Productivity
8.	% Time spent in each phase of SDLC
9.	% Slippages detected in each phase of SDLC

17. Project Closure

1.	Project Details
2.	Things went right
3.	Things went wrong
4.	Learnings from the project
5.	Project Analysis/Post Mortem

Chapter 3

Software Development Models and Approaches

Over a period of time different software development models and approaches have evolved like,

1- Prototyping
2- Iterative
3- Incremental
4- Spiral
5- Waterfall
6- Agile
7- Test Driven Development

3.1 Prototyping

In case of Prototyping, the overall requirements in terms of user interface, look and feel, screens, reports generated, other subsystems invoked etc. are demonstrated to customer without detail implementation.

Prototype gives customer good idea about the systems and also chance to add, modify or remove requirements.

Prototype serves as useful milestone to speed up the work of development and brings more clarity before massive development is done.

The prototypes are of two types,

1. Throwaway Prototype
2. Reusable Prototype

In case of Throwaway prototype all existing design, code is scrapped and better elegant design is detailed out without having any bias towards earlier work done.

In case of Reusable prototype, lot of earlier work is reused.

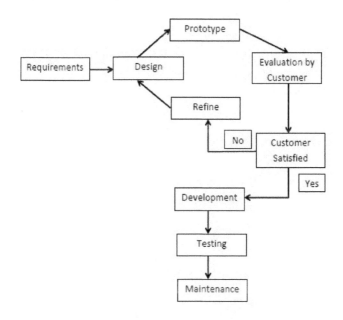

<u>Figure 3.1 Software Prototyping Model</u>

3.2 Iterative

Iterative development involves deviation from traditional Waterfall model steps of development over the product completion.

The development steps can even overlap with each other; if you doing are integration testing you may start work on new requirement or design.

You don't complete a requirement in one go, you keep on iterating till software system or product is fully done.

The Iterative model the development is repetitive and creates new versions of the product, for every iteration.

Every iteration includes the development of a new component of the system which is added to the functionality developed earlier.

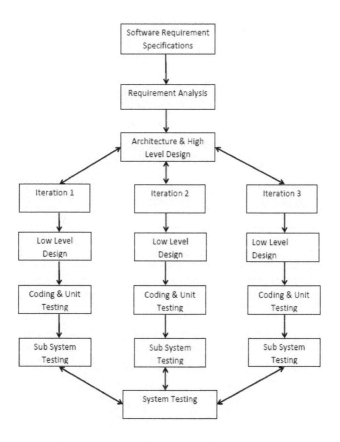

Figure 3.2 Iterative Model of Software Development

3.3 Incremental

Incremental model of software development applied waterfall model steps in iterative manner. Multiple releases are made called as increments which keeps on adding more functionality progressively for each increment developed.

Incremental model of software development goes through the linear sequences over a period of time. Each linear sequence results in an increment with more and more functionality.

In incremental approach "core' system is designed and implemented, and then additional functionality is implemented in series of further overlapping project requirements. The aim is to manage risk by defining and developing a small part of the system at a time.

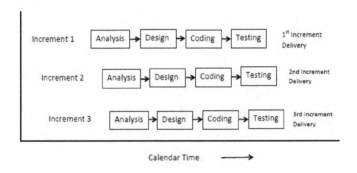

Figure 3.3 Incremental Model of Software Development

Iterative vs. Incremental Development

In iterative development you are adding each time new features whereas in incremental development you are refining things done earlier.

Incremental development means you decide on your product roadmap and then implement features incrementally.

In incremental development you just build as much as you need. You don't over sophisticate them unless essential. When the need is felt, you will build on the top of whatever already exists.

NASA's Apollo program involved iterative and incremental missions. The first mission, Apollo 11 was to land a man on the Moon in 1969. Each new NASA mission, from 1 to 11, gone through incremental approaches of experimentation and iterative improvement in gradual manner.

Development of browsers like Google Chrome and Mozilla Firefox used iterative and incremental software development.

Therefore iterative development need not be incremental and vice versa.

3.4 Spiral

This method of development combines iterative development with systematic controlled waterfall model with emphasis on risk analysis.

Spiral model is more focused on risk analysis. It goes through loops of development in spiral manner like planning, risk analysis, engineering, and evaluation.

In case of Spiral model, often called "Design Little, Do Little", an approach is such that instead of complete 100% design only partial design is done at a time and the same is implemented, demonstrated and further design and development is carried out.

This approach has many benefits of better evolving design which is flexible at each stage and can accommodate better changes than traditional waterfall approach.

This method is suitable for large, expensive and complex projects.

This is a costly model and needs deep expertise in risk analysis and not suitable for simpler projects.

There are many loops in spiral of development and each loop involves software development. Each loop goes thru gradual releases and refinements along with prototyping at each phase.

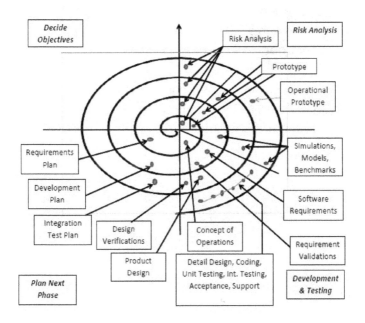

Figure 3.4 Spiral Model of Software Development

3.5 Waterfall

In case of Waterfall model, all software development stages are done sequentially one after another, it's useful when system requirements are very well understood and need no changes.

In this approach better control on the project execution can be kept, as better planning can be done for all stages in effective manner.

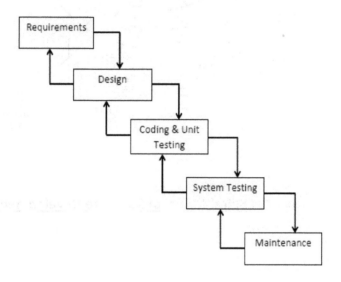

Figure 3.5 Waterfall Model of Software Development

3.6 Agile

There is no fixed standard for doing agile development. There are some agile methodologies like Scrum, XP, Kanban because they follow similar approaches in development. Early client feedback, regular client interaction, frequent releases and frequent demos, evolving design, etc. are the part of Agile development and thus they can be iterative and incremental.

Agile keeps focus on releasing "potentially usable product" after every sprint. Sprint is small duration development cycle of few days or weeks.

Agile development has main focus on absorbing changes suggested by client on regular basis to avoid last minute feedback.

Agile development uses both Incremental and iterative development as a part of an agile development strategy.

3.7 Agile Project Management with Scrum

Scrum is a methodology of Agile development. Scrum team has three members.

Product Owner

This person tried to maximize the value of development team efforts. He/she has right product backlog and with right priority.

Software Development Team

Development team consist of few members and they select the user stories as per product owner priority and then they try to complete in the best manner they feel.

Scrum Master

Scrum master works along with product owner, development team and ensure that scrum process is followed.

Scrum consists of various Sprints of short durations with clear goals by taking features from product backlog and completing them.

Proper Sprint planning is involved in terms of Sprint goal and way to accomplish it.

There are daily stand up meeting in development teams called Daily Scrum meetings to discuss what was done previous day and what is the focus for today and any risks if they see.

Each Sprint ends with Sprint review to review the progress and future Sprint planning.

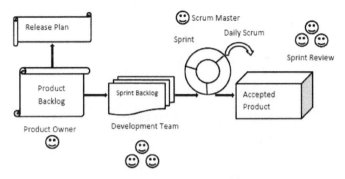

Figure 3.6 Agile Software Development with Scrum

3.8 Test Driven Development (TDD)

Test Driven Development (TDD) is one of the types of software development process in which the end user functionality is well understood in granular fashion first and then the granular unit test cases are written by testing team by close interaction with the customer. These unit test cases are then used by developers to write the code to implement the functionality.

This is a reverse process as compared to traditional way of developing the code, then writing the test cases and executing them. Since in test driven development code is focussed on passing the unit tests, the amount of code generated is small and not bulky. When the tests are executed and if the code fails then the code is refactored and tests are executed again, this cycle repeats. This type of development leads to cohesive code and loose coupling. During the refactoring proper code clean-up is done and code is also optimized. The tests written forms the part of regression test suite.

The following sequence of steps is generally followed:

- Add a test
- Run all tests and see if the new one fails
- Write some code
- Run tests
- Refactor code
- Repeat

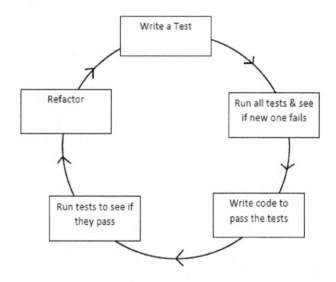

<u>Figure 3.7 Test Driven Software Development (TDD)</u>

There are two other approaches related to test driven development, they are ATDD (Acceptance Test Driven Development) and BDD (Behavior Driven Development).

In ATDD the developers focus on writing code which will meet the acceptance criteria and in BDD the focus of tests is on the behaviour of the system rather than unite tests for unit of implementation.

BDD combines TDD and ATDD and needs close interaction between developers, testing team and business people.

Advantages of TDD

- High quality code generation in short time
- Since there is a close interaction and good knowledge of system functioning the code quality is high
- TDD created Regression test suite which helps in automated test
- Early fixes due to early functionality test based development
- Generated minimum code
- Cohesiveness of code
- Lose coupling of code

Disadvantages of TDD

- Skills required are high
- Isolation of components may not be easy to begin with
- Tests to be properly maintained
- Initial development is slow due to unit test creation
- Quality of code depends on the quality of tests written

Chapter 4

Quality

What is Quality? There are many definitions of Quality. In ISO 8402 Quality is defined as "The totality of features and characteristics of a product, process or service that bear on its ability to satisfy stated or implied needs".

4.1 Quality Attributes

There are functional and non-functional attributes which makes a software.

The functional attributes are directly related to visible software, whereas non-functional attributes are the one which are applicable to the various work products which gets generated during a SDLC e.g. Specifications, Design, Code, Test Plans, Documentation etc.

It is important to note that your client needs good quality software and that means he/she must get high quality of functional and non-functional attribute quality and not just functional or not just non-functional attribute quality.

How to define Quality attributes is debatable topic. There are different approaches which have been discussed in this area. One approach is to refer to, In

"Characteristic of Quality", by Barry Boehm et al. (1978) report on study done at TRW for the US National Bureau of Standards in 1973. The various attributes mentioned are,

1. Reliability
2. Efficiency
3. Portability
4. Human Engineering
5. Testability
6. Understandability
7. Modifiability

The above attributes in turn consist of one to many of the following attributes,

1. Device Independence
2. Completeness
3. Accuracy
4. Consistency
5. Device Efficiency
6. Accessibility
7. Communicativeness
8. Structuredness
9. Self-descriptiveness
10. Conciseness
11. Legibility
12. Augmentability

The second approach to quality attribute is as defined by Tom Glib in the technique he refers to as "design by objectives" (1987). Here Glib uses a technique in which quantifiable as well as unquantifiable attributes are made testable and measurable by refinement.

Each attribute is decomposed to the extent it can be measured, once the decomposition is done Glib recommends for each attribute to specify,

1. Measuring concept
2. Measuring tool
3. A worst permissible value
4. A planned value
5. The best value
6. Today's meaningful value

4.2 Factors to Judge the Quality

In software projects and/or products quality can be judged by various factors, some are as given below, there can be many more.

1. Number of requirements or features fully developed as per the specification
2. Partially developed requirements or features
3. Number of defect observed during acceptance testing phase
4. Number of defects observed in usage post acceptance phase
5. Ease of use
6. Workflow not as per the definition
7. Number of critical defects
8. Number of major defects
9. Number of minor defects
10. Installation errors
11. Errors in documents delivered, quality of documentation
12. Quality of training
13. Quality of trainers
14. Quality of support
15. Delay in support

Various tools are available to log the above defects so that they can be verified by Quality Engineering (QE) team and then if the defects are seen then the development team can prioritize and address them.

Chapter 5

Quality Systems

The software engineering needs well defined documented Quality Systems in the organizations. To bring out some consistency in the framework of these documented systems, different Quality Systems emerged like ISO 9001, SEI CMM (Software Engineering Institute Capability Maturity Model) etc. The different auditing companies exist today which can certify if a given documented Quality Systems complies with ISO 9001 or as per SEI CMM.

ISO 9001 is more in line with manufacturing practices whereas SEI CMM is more suitable towards software development activities.

An organization needs to decide which Quality System they should adopt and define their practices in line with decided system and get certified from proper certifying authorities.

5.1 ISO 9001

ISO 9001 is identical to BS 5750 (1987) and the proposed European Standard EN29000. ISO 9001 can be implemented as Quality Management Systems in any industry, so while using it for software organization, few things need to be focused from software angle.

ISO 9001 defines following 20 major requirements,

1. Management responsibility
2. A documented quality system
3. Contract review
4. Design control
5. Documentation and change control
6. Purchasing
7. Purchaser supplied product
8. Product identification and traceability
9. Process control
10. Inspection and testing
11. Inspection, measuring and test equipment
12. Inspection and test status
13. Control of nonconforming products
14. Corrective action
15. Handling, storage, packaging and delivery
16. Quality records
17. Internal quality audits
18. Training
19. Servicing
20. Statistical techniques

5.2 CMMI (Capability Maturity Model Integration)

This is a process level improvement and appraisal program. Various levels defined in CMMI are as below,

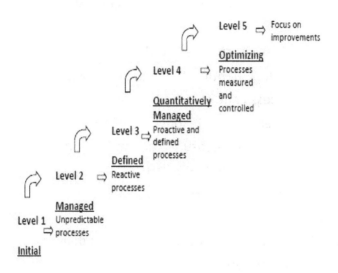

Figure 5.1 Five Levels in CMMI

It was developed by Carnegie Melon University (CMU) and many US contracts ask for CMMI assessment while giving contracts to vendor.

It has different versions which are released from time to time, CMMI 1.3 was released in 2013 and CMMI 2.0 was released on 2018.

The Quality Systems though initially looks like an overhead it pays for itself in due course of time, it brings process orientation within an organization and predictability and repeatability to deliver quality and on time, and this is the sole purpose of Quality System.

In absence of these systems the organization may still have process to follow but a formal certification in case of ISO 9001 and assessment in case of SEI CMM is highly recommended.

These certification or assessments do help in increasing customer confidence in order to deliver quality and in time from the outsourced company. Many end user companies don't recommend or outsource work to those IT services companies who are not having any certification.

The essence of certification or assessment is not just certification or assessment but final end quality of deliverables, this aspect must be kept in mind, these are the means to an end but not an end in itself.

Regular audits to gauge and measure the quality and improvements in quality must be carried out to make quality as an ultimate goal. Various steps must be taken to optimize the quality achieved.

Looking at the above top management must ensure and support all the initiatives to get certification, in the long run if you want to compete, it will be an asset.

Chapter 6

Business Requirements, Functional Requirements and Software Requirement Specifications

6.1 Business Requirements

Business requirements are essential part of any software development. They are captured as Business requirement document (BRD).

BRD document is useful throughout the project life cycle to ensure that all the deliverables meet business and customer needs.

BRD focuses on business angle and business perspective to develop a system for addressing a given business solution. It talks about client needs and expectations. BRD talks about what business really needs.

BRD highlights all project deliverables.

Focus of BRD is objectives of business and is different from business solution and technical solution.

6.1.1 Business Requirement Document (BRD) Objectives

- To bring common understanding across all stakeholders
- Details to be given to technology solution provider in terms of business needs and client needs
- Input and output from each phase

6.1.2 Contents of Business Requirements Document (BRD)

Business analyst or domain expert or subject matter expert who understands business processes well creates the business requirement document. BRD is used by the project team.

BRD highlights scope of project, constraints and limitations.

The scope consists of:

- Business problems to be addressed
- Limitations
- Time and efforts to be spent are if really worth for the project spent and efforts

6.1.3 BRD Template

The BRD template contains the followings:

- Statement of summary
- Objectives of project
- Statement of business and client needs
- Scope of project
- Financial statements
- Functional requirements
- Resource needs
- Schedule
- Assumptions
- Cost & Benefits

6.2 Functional Requirements

Functional Requirement describes software components of the system. Each function has input, output and processing logic. It often focuses on business logic or processes, user interactions, data manipulations etc.

Functional Requirements are also called as **Functional Specification**.

Functional specifications address the intended behaviour of the system.

6.2.1 Functional Requirements Document (FRD)

Functional Requirement Document describes all the functions required to meet the business need.

BRD explains *what business wants* whereas the FRD talks about *how the business needs* can be achieved.

FRD is created based on BRD.

Functional Requirement	Description
F-Req 1	e.g. Enter inventory data
F-Req 2	e.g. Generate bar charts
F-Req-3	e.g. Generate report of inventory

Functional Requirements covers the followings:

- Each screen input
- Business logic
- Output from the system
- Data handling logic
- System reports
- Workflows performed by the system
- Users allowed to create/modify/delete the data in the system
- Regulatory and compliance needs

6.2.2 Functional Requirement Benefits

Various benefits are:

- Keeps track of all the functionalities mentioned in the functional requirement of the application
- Explains the functionality of a system or subsystems
- Helps to identify missing requirements during the analysis
- Defines the expected system service and behavior
- Helps to catch the errors in the Functional requirement stage
- Focuses on customer goals, needs, processes, tasks and activities

6.2.3 Functional Requirements Types

Some of the most often types of functional requirements are:

- Business logic
- Data management
- Transaction details
- Reports required
- Certification Required
- Authenticated users
- Authorized users
- Administrative users and functions
- Audit trail
- Interfaces
- Compliance required
- Regulatory Requirements

6.2.4 Non Functional vs. Functional Requirements

There are various non-functional requirements also; some of them are as given below:

- Quality
- Usability aspects
- Performance of the system
- Scalability
- Security aspects

6.2.5 Functional Requirement Key Recommendations

Some the key recommendations of functional requirement are as follows:

- Granularity of requirement is important
- Completeness of each requirement
- Accuracy of each requirement
- Cover all technical requirements
- Cover all the objectives of the system
- Use different modes to capture all the requirements by proper dialog with end users
- All the constraints affecting the systems performance
- Assumptions
- Don't put unwanted extra details
- Map the requirements to the objectives

6.3 Software Requirements Specification (SRS)

A software requirements specification (SRS) explains *what the software system will do and how it should perform.*

SRS helps to carry out the software development work faster to reduce the time and cost of development.

SRS mentions all the interactions like:

- Human interaction
- Hardware interaction
- Interactions with other programs or systems

All the non-functional parameters are also captured like:

- Operating system
- Speed,
- Portability,
- Maintainability

IEEE (Institute of Electrical and Electronics Engineers) describes SRS by its specification number 830-1998.

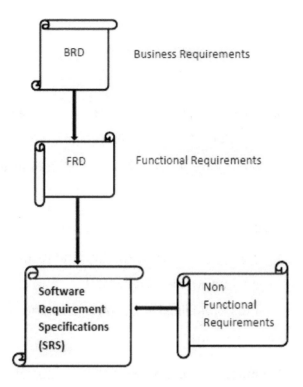

Figure 6.1 SRS creation from BRD and FRD

6.3.1 SRS Important Sections

The various important sections of a software requirements specification are as follows:

- **Business Drivers**: Here *why the need of system* is described, if an old system exist then *why new system* is required and *how it will be better* than old system is described.

- **Business Model:** In this section business model is described. Business functions and process flow is documented.

- **Business/Functional and System Requirements:** In this section all the business requirements/functional requirements are mentioned and detail system requirements are listed.

- **Business and System Use Cases:** In this section various use cases are described and various entities interacting are described. Methods like UML (Unified Modeling Language) are used to create use case diagrams.

- **Technical Requirements:** In this section all technical requirements are listed down to address the technical environment under which software will be operated to operate and also various technical restrictions.

- **System Qualities:** In this section all the non-functional requirements like scalability, availability, reliability, serviceability, security and maintainability to meet the quality attributes.

- **Constraints and Assumptions:** In this section any constraints on the system design and development team's assumptions for the project development are mentioned.

- **Acceptance Criteria:** In this section all the expected functioning required during the execution of developed software so that end user will accept the system are mentioned.

6.3.2 Purpose of SRS

An SRS defines a document which is agreed amongst all the stakeholders and which is used during the development by all the stakeholders, like software development, operations, quality engineering and maintenance.

SRS speeds up the development work and reduces the time and cost of development.

6.3.3 SRS in Agile development

In Agile development brief documents are created like user stories and acceptance criteria.

In this approach close interaction with end user happens and close working is established between those creating user stories and end user.

6.3.4 SRS Template

SRS template can cover the sections as given below:

Table of Contents

5. System Performance Requirements

6. Non-functional Requirements

6.1 Scalability
6.2 Reliability
6.3 Maintainability
6.4 Portability
6.5 Extensibility
6.6 Reusability
6.8 Security

7. Operational Details and Scenarios

8. Use Case Models and Sequence Diagrams

8.1 Use Case Model
8.2 Sequence Diagrams

9. Important Milestones and Delivery Schedule

10. Appendix

6.4 Good Requirement Specifications

The importance of a good requirement specification can't be undervalued. This is a very important phase of capturing client requirements and translating for the other phases of SDLC, especially Architecture, Design, Testing etc.

This is a very important activity and errors in this phase have great impact on final deliverables to client, the quality of deliverable and timeliness of deliverables. If the requirements are not up-to the mark, client gets many surprises at later phases of SDLC and it cost a lot to make the corrections at project completion stage.

6.4.1 Properties of Good Requirement Specifications

A good requirement specification should have following properties,

1. Unambiguous
2. Complete
3. Consistent
4. Implementable
5. Verifiable
6. Validatable
7. Modifiable
8. Understandable
9. Testable
10. Traceable

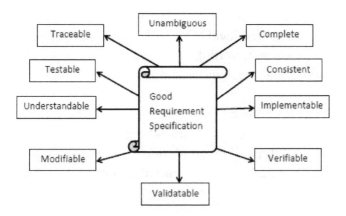

Figure 6.2 Properties of Good Requirement

Figure 6.2 Properties of Good Requirement Specifications

Let us look at the above properties in brief.

1. Unambiguous

The requirements should be clear and unambiguous so that there is no confusion across all the stakeholders. The requirements should be documented and should be sent to client for review or should be presented to remove any gaps in understanding.

At times usage of prototyping or a pilot can serve very useful exercise, e.g. "We need good GUI" is an ambiguous statement, and it has to be detailed out what it means to be a good GUI, what will define good GUI etc.

2. Complete

The requirements should be complete and captured in as much micro level as possible. All the required inputs to the system, outputs from the system, processing logic etc. are well discussed in detail.

A statement like "The exact format for the required report will be given in future" is a case of incompleteness. Incomplete requirements cause lot of reword due to impact on architecture or design or code written.

3. Consistent

Each requirement and micro functionality should be consistent and to be interpreted in uniform manner throughout the requirement specification document so that there is no scope for multiple interpretations and possible errors in development of a system.

4. Implementable

Each requirement must be implementable, it should not be hypothetical such that after it has been agreed and found to be non-implementable will lead to conflict during acceptance and contract closure. If some requirements are likely in such category , a proof of concept must be carried out by telling customer in advance and should be accepted only if found implementable or otherwise there is a need to modify the requirement to meet the business need.

5. Verifiable

The requirements should be such that they can be verified after the implementation or even at early stage of architecture, details design phase, in absence of such the development and acceptance becomes difficult and can lead to many contractual issues during closure.

Statement like " Speed will be good and response time will be faster " is a non-verifiable statement as speed and response time depends on many factors and unless those are defined, requirement cannot be completely verifiable.

6. Validatable

The client should be in position to validate objectively all that he/she has spelled to develop is exactly captured otherwise subjectivity and ambiguity prevails and cause delays during development and delivery of a work product.

7. Modifiable

All said and done some requirements are likely to change during the course of development, as all of them might not be fully freezable at early stage and some may evolve subsequently, however these requirements should not be such that they have tremendous impact on the whole architecture and/or design.

A sizable cushion to absorb some changes is a pragmatic expectation and reality with which we need to live.

8. Understandable

Different people who participate in a project consist of client, architects, analyst, designer, developers, testers, end users, documenters etc. All need to interact in one way or another and everyone has different style of communication.

The requirements should be easy to understand to various participants. e.g. "Parent Class Employee will have name, age, address", a statement like this may not be understandable to the recipient of the system or a non-developer, but may to the designer and developer.

9. Testable

All that gets developed gets accepted provided testing results are found acceptable to the client, therefore the requirements have to be testable so that after the development is done they can be said to be OK or not OK, and all possible test scenarios should give the results as expected.

10. Traceable

During a SDLC, one phase has effect on next succeeding phase hence the requirements have to be traceable, each requirement can be mapped to design, testing etc., it makes impact analysis and change management very controllable.

The above properties have to be fulfilled while requirements are detailed out and efforts should be made that no gaps exist between client's expectations and deliverables, if this happens the speed of development is much faster, time to deliver is minimal and quality of final software will be high.

Chapter 7

Software Analysis and Design

Software analysis and design includes all activities which transform requirement specifications into implementation.

Requirement specifications consist of all functional and non-functional requirements.

Methodologies for Software Analysis and Design

Different methodologies have evolved over the last few years as the software development processes matured, new development technologies and development languages evolved and time to deliver as early as possible became a necessity.

Also skills, ease of development, constraints, available tools, maintenance aspects of software and how reusability can be utilised has impact on software analysis and design methodologies.

There are mainly two methodologies as given below:

1. Structured System Analysis and Design Method (SSADM)
2. Object Oriented Analysis and Design (OOAD)

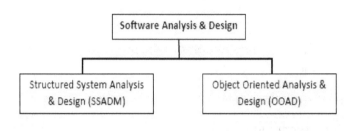

Figure 7.1 Methodologies of Software Analysis and Design

7.1 Structured Systems Analysis and Design Method (SSADM)

Structured system analysis and design methodology (SSADM) consist of standards for structured software analysis and design. It uses formal methodologies to address analysis and design.

Learmonth Burchett Management Systems (LBMS) and the Central Computer Telecommunications Agency (CCTA) in 1980-1981 introduced this as a standard for developing British database projects.

The SSADM is a methodology based on the waterfall model. It has been widely used by many developers, businesses, consultants, educational institutes and CASE tool developers.

SSADM is highly dependent on deep user involvement in the requirements specifications stage. The requirements are signed off by the end users. The requirements are well documented using data flow diagrams etc.

SSADM splits a development project into various stages, modules, steps and tasks.

Data model plays very important role in SSADM.

The technique used in SSADM uses logical data modeling, data flow modeling and entity behaviour modelling techniques.

- **Logical Data Modeling:** This step focuses on identification, modeling and documenting data to address the system requirements. The data consist of many entities and relationships.

- **Data Flow Modeling:** This covers data flow in a system. Analysis of processes, data stores, external entities and data movement is carried out.

- **Entity Behaviour Modeling:** Various events influencing entities and sequence of these events are captured in this process.

7.1.1 Important Characteristics of SSADM

- Splitting a system into small modules with clearly defined objectives
- Useful in requirements specification and system design stage
- Diagrammatic representation and modeling techniques
- Simple and easy to understand for the clients and developers
- Sequence of various performing activities

7.1.2 Stages of SSADM

- Feasibility study
- Study of current environment
- Deciding business systems options
- Requirements definition
- Technical system options
- Logical design creation
- Physical design creation

All the above stages apply techniques and a sequence of analysis. Various procedures are used to record and interpret the system details using diagrams and text.

Use of CASE tools is recommended.

7.2 Object Oriented Analysis and Design (OOAD)

OOAD in software engineering is an iterative and incremental process. Analysis models (for OOA) and Design models (for OOD) are the output created in OOAD.

The OOA and OOD are continuously refined to address the business value and risk.

OOAD is a technical approach to address the analysis and design of a software system using object oriented languages and visual modeling during the software development process to meet the product quality desired and communicates with all the required stakeholders.

Some of the early object oriented methodologies were introduced in mid-1990 by Grady Booch, Peter Coad, James Rumbaugh, Ivar Jacobson, Robert Martin etc.

Various methodologies by the above experts finally merged into Rational Unified process (RUP) covering iterative and incremental development.

Modularity and reusability is an important underlying factor in OOAD.

The real life objects are mapped as classes, each class has methods, some private, and some public, there are interfaces to each class etc. The development goes through the abstract definition of problem and then design to coding, testing and implementation.

OOA creates the model of system of functional requirements without bothering about low level implementation.

In OOAD behaviour (processes) and state (data) are modelled together with real life object philosophy which is not the case in SSADM.

Object models and use cases are used as models in OOA Object models have classes, names, sub classes, operations, properties etc.

Analysis models are mapped to implementation classes in OOD phase and interfaces to make solution domain model.

7.2.1 Object Oriented Modeling (OOM)

Object oriented Modeling (OOM) is an approach to model application, systems, business domains in object oriented manner based on OOA and OOD approach of OOAD.

Object oriented Modeling addresses two aspects of behaviours, dynamic and static. Business processes and use cases are dynamic behaviours and classes and components makes static structures.

Unified Modeling Language (UML) and SysML are the most commonly used standard modelling languages in OOAD based development.

7.3 Unified Modeling Language (UML)

Unified Modeling Language (UML) is a commonly used modelling language to visualize the system design.

This is not a programming language. UML describes the behaviour and structure of a system.

UML is useful in analysis, design and modelling.

Object Management Group (OMG) in 1997 adopted UML as a standard. ISO also approved it in 2005.

Now days multiple teams work on a software system and there is a need for proper communication amongst them. Business people like to understand the system in non-technical language and manner.

The visual modelling brings common and easy understanding and saves lot of time in the development.

UML is best suited for object oriented analysis and design. Various elements of system and their association in the form of diagram help to represent the system.

There are two types of diagrams in UML.

1. Structural Diagrams
2. Behavioural Diagrams

7.3.1 Structural Diagrams

These diagrams represent the **static aspects** of the system and comprises of Component diagrams, Object diagrams, Class diagrams, Composite structure diagrams, Deployment diagrams and Package diagrams.

7.3.2 Behavioural Diagrams

These diagrams cover the **dynamic aspects** or behaviour of the system. These diagrams comprises of Use Case Diagrams, State Diagrams, Activity Diagrams and Interaction Diagrams. UML 2.2 has below hierarchy of diagrams.

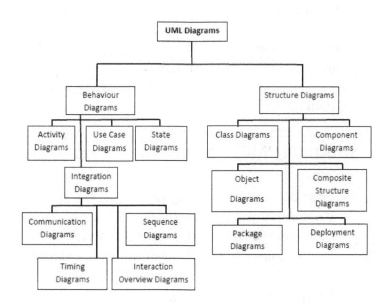

Figure 7.2 UML Diagrams

Object Oriented Concepts Used in UML

1. **Class:** A class defines the structure and functions of an object.
2. **Objects:** An object is the building block of a system which is used to depict an entity.
3. **Inheritance:** Inheritance means child classes inherit the properties of their parent classes.
4. **Abstraction:** implementation details are hidden from user.
5. **Encapsulation:** Data Binding and protecting it from outside world is encapsulation.
6. **Polymorphism:** Functions or entities exist in different forms.

UML 2.0 supports the agile development methodology and number of diagrams are increased from 9 to 13 from the old version of UML 1.x, the newly added four diagrams are timing diagram, communication diagram, interaction overview diagram and composite structure diagram.

Structural UML Diagrams

1. **Class Diagram:** Class diagrams depict the static structure of a system by showing system's classes, their methods and attributes and shows the relationship between different classes or objects.

2. **Composite Structure Diagram:** Describes the internal structure of a class and its interaction with other parts of the system. They use parts, ports, and connectors. Collaborations can also be modelled

using composite structure diagrams. They are similar to class diagrams but represent individual parts in detail as compared to the entire class.

3. **Object Diagram:** An Object diagram is a screenshot of the instances in a system and the relationship between them. An object diagram is similar to a class diagram except it shows the instances of classes in the system. Object Diagram represents specific instances of classes and relationships between them.

4. **Component Diagram:** Component diagrams show the physical components in a system. They are used for modelling implementation details. Component Diagrams help us in understanding functional requirements. They are widely used in complex systems. Components communicate to each other through Interfaces.

5. **Deployment Diagram:** Deployment Diagrams are used for system hardware and its software representation. These diagrams show hardware components present and what software components run on them. They are often used when software used is distributed or deployed over multiple machines with different configurations.

6. **Package Diagram:** These diagrams show how packages and their elements have been organized. They show the dependencies between different packages and their internal composition. They are mainly used to organise class diagrams and use case diagrams.

Behaviour UML Diagrams

1. **State Machine Diagrams:** A state diagram represents the condition of the system or part of the system. It represents the behaviour using finite state transitions. State diagrams are also called as **State machines** and **State-chart Diagrams.** State diagram is used to model the dynamic behaviour of a class in response to time and changing external inputs and events.

2. **Activity Diagrams:** They show the flow of control in a system. Various steps involved in the execution of a use case are shown by Activity diagrams to show the sequential and concurrent activities.

3. **Use Case Diagrams:** Use Case diagrams show the functionality of a system or a part of a system. They are used to explain the functional requirements of the system and its interaction with external actors. Use case diagram shows the different scenarios where the system can be used and gives us a high level view of what the system or a part of the system does without getting into the details of implementation.

4. **Integration Diagrams:** These are the models that describe how a group of objects collaborate in some behaviour, typically a single use case. These diagrams are used for describing some type of interactions among the different model elements. This interaction is a part of dynamic behavior of the system.

5. **Sequence Diagram:** These diagrams show interaction between objects in a sequential order.

   They are also called as event diagrams. Sequence diagrams show the order of functioning of objects in a system.

   These diagrams are useful for business people and software developers to document and understand requirements.

6. **Communication Diagram:** A Communication Diagram also known as Collaboration Diagram in UML 1.x is used for sequence of messages exchanged between objects.

7. **Timing Diagram:** Timing Diagram is a Sequence diagram used to show the behaviour of objects over a period of time.

   They show the time and duration constraints which changes states and behaviour of objects in the system.

8. **Interaction Overview Diagram:** An Interaction Overview Diagram depicts sequence of actions and explains the complex interactions into simpler occurrences.

   It is a combination of activity and sequence diagrams.

Chapter 8

Software Architecture

Software architecture is a process to convert various software characteristics also called as quality attributes like scalability, feasibility, flexibility, reusability, and security into a structured solution to meet the technical and the business expectations.

Business requirements and technical requirements consist of many characteristics.

8.1 Software Architecture Characteristics

Software characteristics also called as quality attributes describe the requirements and the expectations of software in business and technical levels.

A software architect has to focus on key characteristics like performance, low fault tolerance, scalability and reliability as some key characteristics.

If budget is a constraint then another characteristic to be considered is the feasibility.

8.2 Software Architecture Patterns

There are many architecture patters like:

- Microservices

- Layered pattern

- Event driven pattern

- Serverless pattern

8.2.1 Microservices Architecture

The Microservices pattern has become very popular off-late and many well-known companies are using it.

Many independent modular services are developed to perform separate tasks and these modules communicate with each other through API.

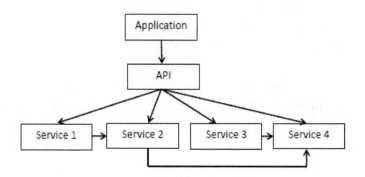

Figure 8.1 Microservices based Software Architecture

8.2.2 Layered Pattern

The application is split into various layers like:

1. Presentation layer
2. Application layer
3. Business layer
4. Persistence layer
5. Database layer

Each layer has its own responsibility and provides service to other upper layer.

The code for presentation layer calls application layer code then application layer code calls business layer code which calls persistence layer code which calls database layer.

Presentation layer deals with user interface, application layer deals is in between presentation and business layer acts as abstraction layer, business layer has all the required business models and the logic.

This architecture is easy to code but builds a monolithic application and lot of unwanted code gets build at each layer.

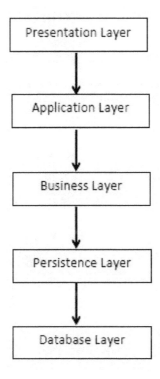

Figure 8.2 Layered Architecture for Software

8.2.3 Serverless Architecture

This refers to application solution that depends on third-party services to manage the servers and management of backend. It consists of "Backend as a service (BaaS)" and "Functions as a Service (FaaS)." The serverless architecture saves lot of time to develop and deploy a system.

The providers for serverless API are Amazon AWS, Microsoft, Google etc.

8.2.4 Event-Driven Architecture

This architecture is based on the Event Producers and Event Consumers. This focuses on decoupling of system parts and each part will be triggered when an event from other part got triggered.

The main idea is to decouple your system's parts and each part will be triggered when an interesting event from another part has got triggered.

Event-producers do not know which event-consumers are listening to which events. Also event-consumers do not know which of them listens to which event-producers.

8.3 Software Architecture vs Design

Software architecture takes care of skeleton and the high-level infrastructure of a software whereas the software design takes care of code level design, what each module is doing, the scope of classes, the functions purposes, etc.

8.4 Software Design Patterns

Design patterns are used as a structured reusable solution and systematically names and explain a general design to address a system design in object-oriented systems. Design patters bring consistency and reduce lot of time to code a system. Repetitive problems and solutions can make best use of design patters.

The often used design patters are:

1. Singleton

2. Factory method

3. Strategy

4. Observer

5. Builder

6. Adapter

7. State

Chapter 9

Software Usability and User Experience (UX)

Usability of software plays very important role in any software. A software may be rich in its features and technology but if the usability of the software to an end user is not satisfactory, the software may not be liked and may not get used to the extent required. In absence of good usability it is also cumbersome to use the software system. Usability engineering is focused on Human Computer Interface (HCI). Usability determines how user friendly the software is.

End user focus is very important and his/her preferences. A proper study of user needs must be carried out to arrive at most optimum usability and user experience for the software.

9.1 Usability Engineering Process

User Experience (UX) and User Interface (UI) must be arrived at on the basis of end user level or personas, how they will use the system, observations of end user, what kind of difficulties they are facing, their suggestions and preferences must be taken into account.

The process will involve the below steps:

- Interacting with user when he/she is interacting with the system
- Testing prototypes
- Getting end user feedback
- Recording their usage, difficulties

Many companies setup their UX lab to carry out the above interactions lively and record the interactions which are then properly analysed to improve and modify the prototype to enhance the usability aspects.

Following steps are carried out:

1. Conducting contextual interviews with end user while they use the system to know their preference, pain points and suggestions.
2. Developing usability specifications based on user needs, competitive analysis and is shared with concerned stakeholders.
3. Development of User interface through iterative process, showcasing at each stage to end user to seek the feedback to improve the UX and UI.

9.2 Usability Specification

In this step all the essential usability attributes are captured. The end users are classified as Personas and each Persona and the features which will be used are noted down and analysed to work out usability specifications.

9.3 Standards

Proper standards in the organization for different platforms like Web, Mobile and Desktop products and solutions must be created so that the same will be used across the organization as a part of UX sustainability and institutionalization.

9.4 Information Architecture

Proper information architecture is carried out to have required features properly logically grouped and their navigation is decided. Focus to be given to have minimum clicks to execute a given workflow.

9.5 Wireframes

Proper wireframes and visual design must be created and shared with development team. The feedback from the development team in implementing or simplifying without compromise in usability is carried out.

9.6 UX Prototype

To validate if the usability specifications will be technically feasible, a prototype might be created and viewed jointly by UX team, development team, end user to firm the specifications. This will help to finalise the UX design.

9.7 Early Feedback from the Field Test

Initial software with user interface and mock up to field users gives important initial feedback before it is implemented by development team to avoid the rework.

During these field test focus should be on the end user feedback, usability and ease of use as felt by end users who can then subsequently test other versions as a part of iterative development to accomplish the goals of high usability aspects.

9.8 Usability Testing

Usability testing is carried out to record the task execution time, end user attitude during the usage, audio and video capturing in audio video mixers to analyse and improve the prototype as well as finish software through regular iterative process.

Users are preferably asked to use the system in target environment or simulated target environment like form factors, screen size, colours etc. and all the observations related to its usage, difficulty, preferences, suggestions, difficulties faced while using the software and suggested improvements are noted.

9.9 Difference between Usability and User Experience

People often do not get clarity as what is usability and what is user experience.

ISO Definition: *Usability is* concerned with the "effectiveness, efficiency and satisfaction with which specified users achieve specified goals in particular environments" (ISO 9241-11) whilst *User Experience* is concerned with "all aspects of the user's experience when interacting with the product, service, environment or facility" (ISO 9241-210).

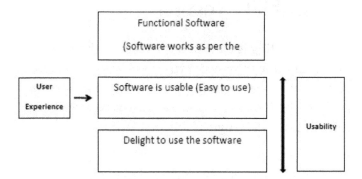

Figure 9.1 Usability vs User Experience (UX)

- **Learnability:** This determines when first time an end user uses the system how easy it was felt by the users to complete the tasks.

- **Efficiency:** Speed of completing the tasks by user once he/she knows the system.

- **Memorability:** How easy to recapture and use the system after it has not used for some time and user goes back to the system to use it again.

- **Errors:** Type of errors, mistakes made by the user while using the system and how fast he/she can recover.

- **Satisfaction:** How much user is satisfied to use the system to complete the tasks?

Chapter 10

Software Testing

Software testing is an important phase of any software development cycle (SDLC) to ensure that developed software is as per the specifications and that there are no defects in the software before it gets delivered to the customer.

Software testing scope covers many areas like,

1. Testing Types

2. Testing Methods

3. Testing Approaches

4. Testing Levels

5. Testing Work-products

10.1 Software Testing Types

There are mainly two types of testing:

1. Manual Testing

2. Automated Testing

10.1.1 Manual Testing

This is a normal manual way of testing the software to verify various functionalities if they are working as per the specifications or not. Proper test plans are created with detailing of each feature testing steps, input to be given, output expected, platform details on which it has to be tested etc.

10.1.2 Automated Testing

Manual testing is slow and laborious. In automated testing various testing tools are used to generate automated tests scripts and they are run during testing so that testing can happen without human intervention and generated test results are stored and analyzed to verify the level of defects and quality.

There are many testing tools like Rational Test Suite, QTP, Selenium etc.

10.2 Testing Methods

1. Static Testing
2. Dynamic Testing

10.2.1 Static Testing

This is a verification phase and includes inspections, reviews and walkthroughs. Various artifacts are verified to ensure that the requirements are proper, other artifacts like architecture, design, test plan, test cases etc. are proper or not to meet the specifications.

10.2.2 Dynamic Testing

In this process software is validated to ensure that it is working as per the requirements specified. It is a dynamic process of testing the actual developed product.

10.3 Testing Approaches

There are three types of software testing approaches.

1. White Box Testing
2. Black Box Testing
3. Grey Box Testing

10.3.1 White Box Testing

White Box testing is based on internal software code of the product built. Various test cases and scenarios are properly coded as a part of unit testing to test the code and do the code coverage.

10.3.2 Black Box Testing

Black Box testing is carried out to test the functionality of software built without getting into the internals of code, design etc. The focus is on expected functioning of software as per the specifications.

10.3.3 Grey Box Testing

Grey box testing is a combination of black box and white box testing. The tester looks at design documents apart from specifications to ensure that level of testing is more deep and spread across to cover as much of developed product as possible.

10.4 Testing Levels

Various testing levels are as follows:

1. Unit Testing
2. Integration Testing
3. Smoke Testing
4. Risk Based Testing
5. Value Based Testing
6. System Testing
7. Acceptance Testing

10.4.1 Unit Testing

Unit testing is focussed on unit level testing, each unit, module or component of software is tested to ensure that they are working as per the specifications or not in the proper development environment.

10.4.2 Integration Testing

Integration Testing involves testing of interfaces, data transfer across the modules. It is carried out as top down or bottom up or hybrid way, combination of top down and bottom up approaches.

10.4.3 Smoke Testing

This is a build verification testing in which most important features are tested to judge the quality of build to be taken ahead for detail testing by spending more efforts. This can be done either in manual testing or automated testing way. This is a non-exhaustive testing. Smoke test helps in identifying integration issues fast and any other major issues. Smoke test gives confidence if it works well or not. If smoke testing fails a new build is asked for again. Smoke test is used in integration testing, system testing and acceptance testing.

10.4.4 Risk Based Testing

In Risk based testing certain amount of risk is taken during testing by focussing on defect prone areas, business criticality, usage frequency, complexity. Important functions, modules, sub systems, components are subjected to test based on importance, impact and chances of failures. When time, resource and budget constraints exist, risk based testing is used.

10.4.5 Value Based Testing

When there is a shortage of resource, time, budget, value based testing is used to get maximum value out of testing efforts. As per Pareto's law, 80% of defects will be detected by 20% of the cases; we need to focus on those 20% test cases to get maximum value out of testing.

10.4.6 System Testing

System testing involves end to end testing of developed software through the black box testing mechanism to ensure that it works as per the specifications. It's a black box testing. Each and every unit, module is tested fully with all kinds of input to verify the output generated and if it is as per the specifications or not. Usability testing is also part of this testing.

10.4.7 Acceptance Testing

Acceptance testing is the final testing either carried out in-house or at customer premises to verify that all features are working and results generated with customer data are as per the specifications, even the speed, performance, scalability, look and feel etc.

10.5 Types of Black Box Testing

1. Functionality Testing
2. Non-functionality Testing
3. Security Testing

10.5.1 Functional Testing

Functional testing is focused on all functional aspects of software and if they are working as per the specifications or not. This is a black box testing. Internal aspects like architecture, design, source code is not looked into by testing people.

10.5.2 Non-Functional Testing

Non-functional testing as the name suggest is focused on non-functional aspects like performance, stress, volume, load, scalability, security, compatibility etc. The user interface, usability aspects are also tested. The responsiveness of the system to varying degree of load is also tested.

10.5.3 Security Testing

Security testing is very important and it ensures safety from outside vulnerabilities like hacking. This involves vulnerability testing, penetration testing and security testing. This type of testing protects the software from external vulnerabilities and increases the confidence of end customer.

10.6 Testing Work-Products

Testing work-products are the work products created in testing phase either shared with end customer or for internal use as a part of SDLC.

Some work products are created before testing begins some during testing and some after the testing is carried out.

Some of the testing artefacts are,

1. Test Strategy
2. Test Plan
3. Traceability Matrix
4. Test Cases
5. Test Scripts
6. Test Suite
7. Test Data

10.7 Software Testing Models

There are different testing models like,

1. Waterfall Model
2. V Model
3. Agile Model
4. Spiral Model
5. Iterative Model

Each of the above models has its own advantages and disadvantages. Depending on the type of software, size of the software, complexity of the software etc. one has to decide which model will suit best.

10.7.1 Waterfall Model

As explained earlier under Waterfall development methodology, testing also follows the sequential phases of SDLC starting with requirement analysis, design, coding, testing, and implementation.

The different phases in the **Waterfall model** are:

- Requirement analysis
- Design phase
- Coding, implementation
- System Testing
- Maintenance

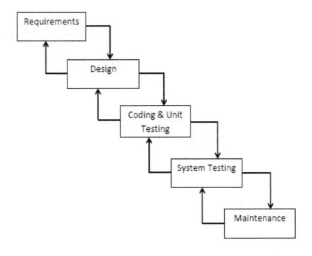

Figure 10.1 Waterfall Model of Software Testing

Benefits

- Easy to implement and maintain
- Verification of requirements and systems helps in the development phase
- Resources requirement is minimal

Disadvantages

- No scope for changing the requirements
- Each next phase has dependency on completion of earlier phase

10.7.2 V Model

The V Model is better than waterfall model. The development and testing activities are carried out side by side.

While business requirements are getting frozen acceptance test plan and cases are created, during software specification phase, system test plan and cases are created, during high level design, integration test plan and cases are created, during low design phase unite test plan and test cases are created.

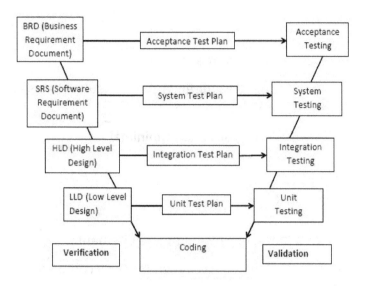

Figure 10.2 V - Model of Software Testing

Benefits

- Easy to use as testing activities like test strategy, planning and test designs are done before the coding phase

- Chances of success are high and saves time

- Defects are detected at early stage

Disadvantages

- Rigidity of the model

- Test artifacts gets impacted due to changes in the design or code

---

10.7.3 Agile Model

In the Agile model as explained earlier there is a close interaction with end user and changes in requirements are easy to adapt, short development cycles with iterative and incremental steps and regular usable products releases for the customer.

The agile software testing model is on the same line of agile development and focuses on rapid delivery of completed software product through various small incremental builds produced in each Sprint cycle.

Product owner created a product backlog. Features are prioritized to get the maximum value from each Sprint cycle in case of Scrum based Agile development.

Each Sprint goes through Discover, Design, Develop and Test steps. After the first Sprint is tested then the second Sprint will be taken for the testing. This is repeated to cover all the Sprints.

Each Sprint creates a finished demonstrable and/or usable product due to close interaction between customer and the development team.

Scrum is managed by a Scrum Master and there are daily meetings to review the progress and plan the remaining work.

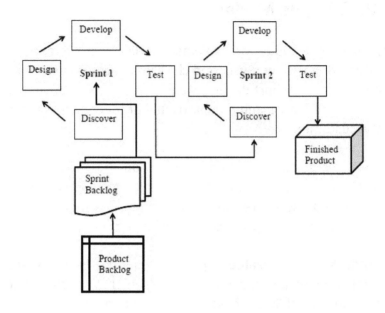

Figure 10.3 Agile Model of Software Testing

Benefits

- Rapid and continuous development of deliverables
- Customer satisfaction
- Flexible model
- Quick development and adaptation to changing requirements

Disadvantages

- Efforts required for large and complex software development difficult to estimate

- Frequent changes asked by customer can impact the development

10.7.4 Spiral Model

Spiral model is more focused on risk analysis. It goes through loops of development in spiral manner like planning, risk analysis, engineering, and evaluation.

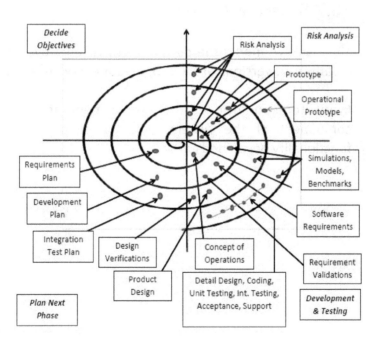

Figure 10.4 Spiral Model of Software Testing

Benefits

- Suitable for complex and large systems
- Functionalities can be added during development

Disadvantages

- Costly model and needs deep expertise in risk analysis
- Not suitable for simpler projects

10.7.5 Iterative Model

The Iterative model the development is repetitive and creates new versions of the product for every iteration.

Every iteration includes the development of a new component of the system which is added to the functionality developed earlier.

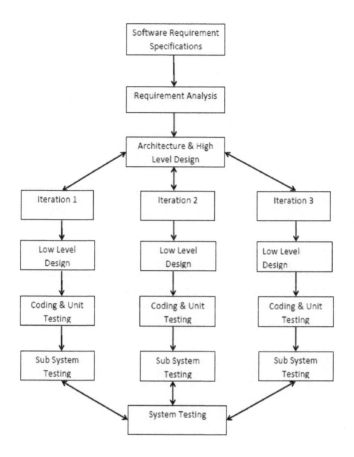

Figure 10.5 Iterative Model of Software Testing

Benefits

- Easy to control the risks as high-risk tasks are addressed first

- Progress is easy to measure

- Risks, issues detected in one iteration can be avoided in the next iteration

Disadvantages

- More resources required than waterfall model
- Sometimes the process is difficult to manage
- Risks may not be known even at the final stage of development

Chapter 11

Software Configuration Management (CM)

Software Configuration Management deals with proper tracking of all configurable items through software development cycle (SDLC) to manage, organize and control them.

A configurable item is a one which needs to be controlled and goes through the modifications by authorized people only.

Software Configuration management needs well defined policies, procedures while using configuration management tools which are necessary to manage the revisions through SDLC to various configurable items along with tracking revision history and status.

11.1 Benefits of Configuration Management

Proper configuration management will help for the followings:

- Less errors and less confusion in terms of using right work-products

---

- Efficiency in development

- Multiple people across multiple geographies can work parallely

- Co-ordination amongst the stakeholders

- System compliance as per defined established specifications and guidelines

- Proper checks in place to modify control documents
- Proper governance on configurable items

11.2 Configuration Management Steps

Configuration management goes through the following five steps:

1. Plan

2. Identify Configurable Items

3. Control Records

4. Status Accounting

5. Audit and Reviews

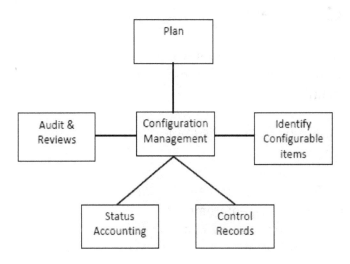

Figure 11.1 Software Configuration Management Steps

11.2.1 Plan

When in any software development a project plan is prepared, configuration management is initiated. Configuration management plan forms the part of project management plan. It can follow IEEE 828 or other standard as decided in the organization.

The configuration management processes and the approach are well described and documented so that everyone is aware of configuration management process, tools, methodology and approach. This plan needs to be approved by project manager.

11.2.2 Identify Configurable Items

Every configurable item which needs control and proper modification process needs to be uniquely identified for the tracking.

Various types of configurable items are:

- Project Plan
- Business requirement document
- Functional requirements
- Software requirement specifications
- Architecture
- Design
- Coding standard
- Documentation templates
- Manuals
- Client data
- Documents supplied by client
- Signed off documents
- Artefacts which needs limited access for security by limited people

Configuration management is a dedicated job assigned to configuration manager or one of the people on project who owns this as his/her responsibility.

11.2.3 Control Records

All the configuration items need to be controlled to ensure that there is a proper audit trail from the initial version to the finally done version.

A proper baselining procedure is followed. A proper versioning process is followed. Proper security and unwanted changes by multiple people without systematic merging and reviewed by authorized person is ensured.

11.2.4 Status Accounting

Status accounting provides status of any configurable items as per the access given. As documents goes through the process of creation, work in progress, completed, being reviewed, checked in, checked out etc. are known to the project team.

All the changes in the document or artefacts are recorded so that people will know why some document got changed, by whom so that there is no confusion while using the latest versions.

11.2.5 Audit and Reviews

Configured items are regularly audited to ensure that team is progressing on right track and using the correct latest versions. Software audit team will audit this regularly to bring out any anomalies if found to the project manager.

Configuration management process helps to ensure that all the deliverables used the correct version during SDLC and ensures that no unauthorized people can modify the documents without the knowledge of concerned people.

11.3 Software Configuration Management Tools

Configuration management tools should have following features:

Concurrency Management:

Often the same file is edited by many people. Configuration management tools must provide and manage the concurrency to avoid confusion.

Version Control:

Every modified file on changes and when saved will create a new version. Proper rollback to earlier versions must be supported.

Synchronization:

Synchronization of local version so that correct latest version is used after the changes incorporated by multiple people working on the same document or multiple document along with others.

Chapter 12

Software Release Management (SRM)

Software Release Management is a process of managing, planning, scheduling and controlling software build through different stages and environments including testing and deploying the releases.

Release Management is rapidly growing practice in software engineering. As software development is becoming complex, multi team, multi time zone, many technologies and platforms are being used, it is now essential to have release management as separate dedicated focus and discipline to manage the releases across multiple platforms on regular basis.

More and more software releases are becoming common process due to shorter development cycles, use of Agile methodologies, DevOps and Continuous Delivery mechanism. Continuous integration and continuous delivery have become regular essential part of today's development and more and more automation tools and techniques are available.

Due to the above development scenarios there is a
need for robust software release management process.

12.1 Software Release Management Steps

Software release management is based on following
steps:

1. Release Policy
2. Release Template
3. Release Planning
4. Build Release
5. User Acceptance Testing
6. Prepare Release
7. Deploy Release

12.1.1 Release Policy

This covers release types, standards and governance
requirements for an organization.

12.1.2 Release Template

This consists of all human and automated activities and
follows an organization's release policies.

Figure 12.1 Software Release Management

12.1.3 Release Planning

Release planning takes lot of time and is rigorous to decide the structure of release from the start. Proper release plan is essential to stay on track and serve as a useful standard.

Release plan is based on software development life cycle (SDLC).

Release plan consist of followings:

1. Requirements
2. Overall scope
3. Timelines
4. Delivery schedule

Proper release workflow is to be created and to be presented to all the stakeholders and once finalised it will serve for better control and planning.

12.1.4 Build Release

Development goes through the SDLC steps and builds software to be tested by the Quality Engineering (QE) team.

QE team will test and reports any defects detected which will be fixed by the software development team. This is an iterative process till the release is approved internally.

12.1.5 User Acceptance Testing

User acceptance testing (UAT) is carried by the user and if there are any issues, bugs found are fixed by development team in iterative way till acceptance is achieved. Prior to this rigorous internal testing is completed.

12.1.6 Prepare Release

After all the issues are closed which were found in release in the organization and Quality Review is carried by QE team to ensure that build meets minimum acceptance standard and all the features planned are complete and found working then the release is deployed with proper approval from product owner.

12.1.7 Deploy Release

In this stage release goes on the production environment, all concerned people are informed about the new release.

Any issues post deployment, during deployment stages are discussed with development team to improve the same.

Any issues found must be documented for better communication and tracking to close them.

12.2 Major and Minor Releases

Releases can be minor or major releases.
Minor releases have minor changes and enhancements whereas major releases have important features.

Minor releases are often, major releases are infrequent.

12.3 Release Manager

Release Manager takes the ownership of managing the releases and works closely with product owner, development team, IT staff and operations team while managing various release activities.

Release management processes need to be continuously evolved and optimized, one standard process may not suit across the different software products developed in the organization.

Chapter 13

Software Risk Management

Risk is a possibility of failure or potential loss which may or may not happen during a process.

Losses likely to happen in software development due to lack of information or lack of full information or other factors uncontrollable and unknown at the beginning of software development is a software risk.
The risk can be internal or external.

Internal risks can be controlled while external risks are not under the control.

13.1 Risk Management Process

Risk management is a process to identify the risk, reduce the impact of risk, and reduce the chances of causing the risk and risk monitoring.

Some risks are known upfront e.g. unskilled development team or lack of target hardware to test or insufficient infrastructure etc. Some risks are known e.g. If the design is complete but is it really covering all the non-functional requirements. Some risks are completely unknown e.g. using some tools which client has forced upon and team has no prior experience of using it in a project and due to this possibility of impact is unknown.

Software risk management involves the followings:

1. Defining risk clearly
2. Risk probability identification and its likelihood
3. Loss likely due to a risk
4. Liability likely due to risk

Software risk management consist of following processes:

1. Risk Identification
2. Risk Analysis
3. Risk Planning
4. Risk Monitoring

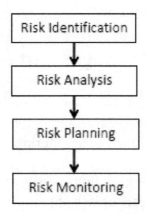

Figure 13.1 Software Risk Management

13.1.1 Software Risk Identification

Identify all the risks likely to happen in a project by studying the scope, various plans, acceptance criteria, skills of the team, tools, and processes used etc. Identify all the internal and external risk likely to cause impact during the execution.

All the risk factor must be thoroughly studied and evaluated which includes technical, operation, political, legal, social factors etc.

Define all the required steps and processes to properly identify the risks. Each risk must be documented along with its details.

13.1.2 Risk Analysis

This is an important aspect of risk management. This addresses the chances of risk likely to happen and its impact to be analysed.

Various factors which can cause the risks can be:

1. Technology to be used
2. Technical skills of the team
3. Communication and understanding within the team members
4. Conflicts
5. Multi-locational teams
6. Multi time zone working of the teams
7. Lack of infrastructure
8. Lack of processes
9. Lack of tools
10. Lack of target environment
11. Lack of proper data in testing

The risk causes the impact, potential loss to a project and organization and the impact need to be accessed in terms of,

1. Loss to the customer
2. Business loss
3. Loss of reputation
4. Loss of client
5. Loss of future business
6. Financial losses
7. Legal impact
8. Contract termination

Risk identified can be low, medium or high.

13.1.3 Risk Planning

Software risk planning consists of:

1. List of all risk
2. Understanding of risk
3. Focus on risk factors
4. Preventive measures to reduce risk happening
5. Measures to reduce the impact due to risk
6. Continuous monitoring to identify risk at the earliest

13.1.4 Risk Monitoring

Risk monitoring is a part of project plan and risk are regularly visited to keep proper checks and control on all identified risks, internal or external.

Software risk monitoring consists of:

- Risk tracking
- Risk review
- Identification of new risk if likely
- Eliminating those risks which are no more valid
- Review the degree of impact of various risks if increased or reduced
- Changes in the priority of risk levels and threats

Software risk management focus on:

- Software failing and not performing as desired
- Software delivery not happening properly

Only software testing will not eliminate the risk. You can monitor what you can measure hence you need to measure and monitor continuously in software development to reduce the risks and their impact.

13.2 Risk Analysis during Software Testing

Risks which cause lot of impact or damages may not be seen earlier. During software testing the type of defects, defect occurrence, density of defects in modules or sub systems or components which are affecting the performance of software must be addressed at the earliest.

Proper test cases, test coverage, testing data, review of test plan, test cases, and skills of testers are all the risks in any software testing and must be monitored continuously.

13.3 Risk Management Models

ISO 31000 is a family of standards related to the risk management defined by International Standard Organization.

Principles and generic guidelines of risk management are defined in ISO 31000:2018.

ISO 31000 family of standards has:

- ISO 31000:2018 – Principles and Guidelines on Implementation

- ISO/IEC 31010:2009 – Risk Management – Risk Assessment Techniques

- ISO Guide 73:2009 – Risk Management – Vocabulary

ISO 21500 Guidance on Project Management standard is also designed to align with ISO 31000:2018 by ISO.

ISO 31000 describes how to deal with risk as given below:

1. Decide not to start or continue with the activity that gives rise to the risk to reduce the risk
2. Accept or increase the risk to seek an opportunity
3. Risk source elimination
4. Change the likelihood
5. Change the consequences
6. Share the risk with another party or parties
7. Informed decision to retain the risk

Chapter 14

Software Support

Once a software is developed and delivered to a customer with proper installation carried out at its site or remotely and once the customer starts using the software after the proper training is imparted, customer often needs support to use the software or faces some issues due to lack of acquaintance of the software.

14.1 Importance of Support

Software support is important to ensure client uses the software optimally and gets all the benefits from the product or system to meet the business needs.

In absence of support the client may find it very difficult to use the software for long and may lose the interest in using the software.

There are different kinds of support provided, some are paid as a part of annual maintenance contract or some are paid as per the use of support provided.

14.2 L1, L2, L3 and L4 Support

There are mainly four types of support L1, L2, L3 and L4 support.

14.2.1 L1 Support

L1 first line support is provided on phone to quickly resolve the client basic issues while using the software.

If the issue can't be resolved then it is escalated to L2 level.

14.2.2 L2 Support

In L2 second line support client complex issues are addressed, client is given workaround if there is an issue to use regular workflow but still customer can do his job to meet the business needs.

If the issue can't be resolved then it is escalated to L3 level.

14.2.3 L3 Support

In L3 third support, immediate fix is not possible hence the issue need to be analysed and its priority is to be decided to be addressed by the development team.

If the issue is very critical and urgent then the development team fixes the issues and may deliver a patch release for the specific customer and if the issue is generic then in that case this fix becomes a part of regular product and all other customers gets the benefit out of it.

14.2.4 L4 Support

In L4 support the help of product vendor and hardware vendor and its engineers help is taken to address the issue.

14.3 Software Support Services

Software support services may include:

1. Remote troubleshooting to resolve the issue
2. Installation related help
3. Usability related help

Remote troubleshooting is provided via telephone and online or without human assistance through already built support applications given to customer or on the company's portal.

Now days automated Robots are built to provide the required support to bring the efficiency and promptness in providing the support for the often asked issues or the problems for which dedicated manpower need not be provided to reduce the cost on 24 X 7 basis.

Software support services may include:

1. Software installation services
2. Software updates installations
3. Major release migrations of software
4. On site proactive or reactive services

---

5. Custom application or infrastructure software support

If the software is custom built then the support is provided by the development agency else if it's a product sold in large number in one country or in many countries worldwide, the support can be from the software product vendor or through nominated third party agencies or partners.

14.4 Software Support Models

Different support models can be provided as per the criticality of application for the customer, size of the software, service level agreements (SLA) etc.

The support models can be:

1. Fully Onsite Model
2. Fully Offshore Model
3. Onsite Centric Model
4. Hybrid Model

In fully onsite model a dedicated team is kept at client location, it is a costly model but fast and prompt and needs minimum co-ordination with offshore team.

Fully offshore support model is for L3 and L4 kind of support, its cost less and response may not be fast like fully onsite model.

Onsite centric model is costly, response is fast, co-ordination with offshore team is for modifications.

In Hybrid model a small onsite team is maintained along with offshore team, simple L2 and L3 issues, workaround etc. can be resolved by onsite team, cost wise this is low in cost.

Chapter 15

Project Management Methodologies

Over the years there are many project management methodologies got developed and evolved. A project manager needs to decide which methodology will suit best while executing a project.

Apart from Waterfall and Agile Methodologies explained in earlier chapters there are few more which are as given below:

1. Critical Path Method (CPM)
2. Critical Chain Project Management (CCPM)
3. Extreme Programming (XP)
4. Adaptive Project Framework (APF)
5. Even Chain Methodology (ECM)
6. Extreme Project Management (XPM)
7. Six Sigma
8. PRINCE2
9. Lean
10. PMI/PMBOK

15.1 Critical Path Method (CPM)

In this method a project work is split into all the tasks along with their duration and dependency on each other to arrive at critical path, slacks within the activities and to arrive at overall project duration. Milestones are arrived at along with list of all deliverables.

The CPM was developed in 1950s by Morgan R. Walker of DuPont and James E. Kelley and was used in the Manhattan Project.

CPM suits more for smaller or mid-size projects.

15.2 Critical Chain Project Management (CCPM)

In CCPM the focus is on all the resources which will be used in the project and not just technology and making optimum use of all resources with proper balancing is the focus.

CCPM was developed by Eliyahu M. Goldratt in 1997 and explained in the book "Critical Path". It is found that with CCPM projects were executed faster and in economical way.

15.3 Extreme Programming (XP)

XP is one of the types of Agile software development with short development cycles and multiple frequent releases to achieve more productivity. Changing customer requirements can be addressed and there is a close interaction during development with client to produce usable software at the end of each short release cycle or sprints. XP has been defined by Kent Beck in 1999.

15.4 Adaptive Project Framework (APF)

APF is flexible and has ability to absorb the client demanded changes. It believes in close client involvement and iterative development.

This methodology is very old though and was introduced by Frederick Taylor in the early 1900s.

15.5 Event Chain Methodology (ECM)

ECM works on the basis of identifying and managing all the events of a project.

It uses CPM and CCPM and has better estimation and scheduling accuracy.

ECM methodology talks about simplifying the risks with project schedules and uses Gantt charts.

It is based on events, risk and activity state, Monte Carlo simulations, chains of critical event, tracking the performance with event chains and event chain diagrams.

ECM is more suitable for projects where there is a great uncertainty during the SDLC throughout the life cycle and can be used across various types of projects.

15.6 Extreme Project Management (XPM)

XPM is focussed on short duration and is flexible. It can address the frequent changes asked by the customer. The short duration plans can be modified regularly as per the need.

XPM addresses the uncertainty in the project. It is a useful way to manage the stakeholders and makes best use of facts gathered and brings more confidence stakeholders.

XPM is suitable for very small duration projects of few days or few weeks.

15.7 Six Sigma

Six Sigma was introduced by Motorola in mid-1980. The focus is on improving quality by identifying what is not working well in the project. It has well defined quality management system and scientific statistics with trained people. Lean Six Sigma methodology was also evolved with focus on eliminating waste.

The focus is on continuous process improvements. This is suitable for large corporations.

15.8 PRINCE2

PRINCE2 means Projects IN Controlled Environments. This is a structured certified methodology. UK government introduced this for IT projects in 1989. PRINCE2 was introduced in 1996 for general project management. It is quite popular project management methodology in UK, Europe, Australia and United Nations.

This is based on six tolerance aspects or KPIs, scope, timescale, risks, quality, benefits and cost.

Project plan addresses scope, timescale and cost. Risk through risk management plan, quality through project product description and benefits through business case are covered.

There are seven principles of PRINCE2, continued business justification, learn from experience, defines roles and responsibilities, manage by stages, manage by exceptions, focus on products and tailor to suit project environment.

It addresses seven themes, business case, organization, quality, plan, risk, change and progress.

PRINCE2 is not recommended for smaller projects.

15.9 Lean

Lean increases the end value delivered and reduces the wastes.

Lean focuses on all the important processes to maximize the value generated. It has a focus to optimize various important resources.

Lean was first used at Ford Car Company by Henry Ford towards the flow production for automating various processes for building cars. Toyota also applied this methodology later.

Lean in software development projects focuses on end user feedback, showing faster prototypes and rapid delivery.

Lean is based on five principles, remove non required steps, and focus on client value, value streams, continuous product movement and effective management at each step.

Lean is useful for those software developments which demands products focused on the end user requirements in cost effective manner with minimal waste.

15.10 PMI/PMBOK

The PMI (Project Management Institute) has published a book PMBOK (Project Management Book of Knowledge) that talks about best practices and guidelines.

Here they talk about project split into five steps i.e. initiating, planning, executing, controlling and closing. Through these steps one can manage and control the project. This also tries to bring uniformity across different types of projects in an organization.

Chapter 16

Project Manager Skills and Training Needs

In today's information technology (IT) and digital world the importance of a good project manager need not be emphasized, it's an important role to make a project success. However there are many IT projects which fail, what can be the reasons? There are many reasons but in absence of a good project manager the possibility to make a project successful is bleak.

16.1 Project Manager Skills Required

What makes a good project manager then?

There are many skills which a project manager must possess, and they are,

1. Domain exposure
2. IT exposure
3. Leadership qualities
4. Good planner
5. Task oriented
6. Team player
7. Should be a catalyst to spur the momentum

8. Ability to gauge risk at every stage and ability to mitigate the risk
9. A good manager
10. Assertive
11. Excellent communicator, oral and written
12. Good listening abilities
13. Ability to comprehend
14. Ability to know all stakeholders
15. Genuine desire to satisfy all stakeholders
16. Client focused
17. Cost conscious

The above are some of the main skills and abilities a successful project manager must have. If you see the above skills you will realize that he/she need not be a hardcore techie guy.

There are good technical experts who can't perform as good project manager and vice versa. One should look at Project Management as an altogether different category and develop right people who want to take role of project management.

16.2 Project Manager Training Needs

There is a heavy shortage of good skilled Project Managers today and organizations must spot the right people who have flair and talent to become good project manager.

They should be given training in various topics like,

1. Project management
2. Project planning
3. Estimation
4. Risk management
5. Client management skills
6. Presentation skills
7. Communication skills
8. Team management
9. Team building
10. Training on project management and tracking

16.3 Project Management Certifications

Certifications like PMP (Project Management Professional), Scrum Master and PMI Agile Certified Practitioner will definitely help.

PMP certification is given by PMI (Project Management Institute) and is recognized as criteria to measure the competency of project managers.

Chapter 17

Project Organization

It's very important to have right organization for each project, often this aspect is neglected considering shortage of skilled manpower and compromises are made to achieve completeness but it ultimately ends up into poor quality and subsequent client dis-satisfaction.

It is often said that the quality of deliverable reflects the underlying project organization used to deliver the project.

The 3Ps of a good project are People, Process and Product (Tools used); this brings out the importance of good people making good software but unless they use right processes and right tools to develop, quality of final deliverables can't be guaranteed.

17.1 Project Organization Structure

Each project must have proper organization in order to succeed. This consist of people like business analyst, planning and control, development team, architects and designers, quality engineering team, configuration management, build/release management team, technical documentation team etc.

Following chart shows typical project organization which can be modified as per the size and complexity of project.

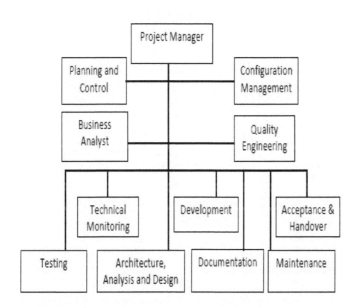

Figure 17.1 Typical Software Project Organization

Once the requirements are frozen, a good estimate of total efforts, phase-wise efforts, relationship between person months and calendar months etc. can be done to formulate right teams for various tasks to be accomplished.

Work breakdown can be done properly and resources can be deployed.

17.2 Commonality between Project Organization and Software Structuring

There are lot of common things between software structuring and project organization structuring as explained below,

Attribute	Software	Project Organization
Unit	Each software unit/module should be small so that it can be well developed.	Each software team to be small so that it can be well controlled.
Coupling	There should exist only loose coupling amongst software units.	Each unit should focus on its own work and should have minimal unwanted communication and dependency on other units.
Cohesiveness	Each software unit should be cohesive so that it delivers its assigned function efficiently.	Work teams must be highly cohesive to work with high efficiency.

Scope division	Each unit should focus on subset of total scope of whole system to be delivered.	Each working team with its lead or manager can make all required decisions for them without affecting other teams.
Hierarchy	Decomposition of system into units to do top level decision functions and actual execution by other units.	Distinction between management staff and execution/imple mentation staff who churns actual implementation tasks.
Connection	Communication links not following hierarchical software structure to be avoided.	In project organization unwanted communication links violating hierarchy to be avoided.

Chapter 18

Software Estimation

Estimation is an important activity in order to arrive at efforts, cost and schedule calculations.

It has been always one of the most and challenging task in a software arena, this is one activity where an organization can lose money if not done properly in fixed price projects.

Estimation has been more of hunch in the past but it has evolved as a proven scientific technique.

The knowledge and expertise on estimation is an asset to any organization.

All those who are involved in bidding stage from technical side must acquire deep knowledge in this area to arrive at good estimates with minimum variations from the actual efforts consumed.

Software Estimation Different Approaches

One should carry out the estimation using many approaches as mentioned hereafter.

18.1 Our Judgement Method (Estimation by hunch)

Split the system into modules and micro level functionality and arrive at approximate coding and unit testing time and apply 20-25% each overheads for Design, Project Management, Testing, and Documentation.

e.g. Coding and Unit Testing Time = 100 days   , then approximately,

Analysis and Design   = 25 days
Project Management = 25 days
Testing   = 25 days
Documentation   = 25 days

Total Time = 200 days

It's a work breakdown method for the estimation but time estimates are by hunch.

18.2 Function Point Analysis (FPA)

This is a method for estimating work contents of software applications which uses an approach other than Lines of Code (LOC). This is based on Functions delivered by software as seen by users.

Function Point (FP) is a unit for measuring size of software applications.

This method was developed by IBM in 1979 and is one of the most popular method.

The advantages of Function Point Analysis are,

- Can be applied at early stages of project
- Evaluation effort is very minimal approximately 1% of project efforts
- Simple to use
- Fast
- Accurate
- Easy to learn
- Easy to understand even to users
- Doesn't need any software tool

The FPA method involves,

- Identification of functions (ILF, ELF, EI, EO, EQ)
- Classification of functions
- Multiplication by weight factors
- Finding sum of raw function points (UFPC)
- Determination of Value Adjustment Factor (VAF)
- Calculation of total adjusted function points (FPC)
- Using organization productivity indices
- Estimation of efforts required

ILF – *Internal Logical File*, a user identified logical related data maintained within the boundary of application.

EIF – *External Interface File*, a user identified logical related data maintained outside the boundary of application.

18.2.1 Transactional Function Types

- **EI** - External Input
- **EO** - External Output
- **EQ** - External Query
- **FP** - Function Point
- **UFPC** - Unadjusted Function Point Count
- **FPC** - Adjusted Function Point Count
- **VAF** - Value Adjustment Factor, it indicates the general functionality provided to the user of application.

VAF comprises of 14 *General System Characteristics* (GSCs) (please refer **Annexure - A**) for more details on GSCs.

For each GSC the *Degree of Influence* (DI) is determined on a scale of 0 to 5 points.

FPC = UFPC * VAF

18.2.2 Complexity Weight Scale

Function Providing Element	Simple	Moderate	Average	Complex	Highly Complex
EI	2	3	4	5	6
EO	3	4	5	6	7
ILF	5	7	10	13	15
EQ	2	3	4	5	6
EIF	4	5	7	9	10

18.2.3 Sample UFPC Calculation

Counts	Functions	Weight	Function Points
8	EI (moderate complexity)	3	24
8	EO (complex)	6	48
3	ILF (average complexity)	10	30
4	EQ (simple)	2	8
3	EIF (highly complex)	10	30

Total unadjusted function points count = 140

18.2.4 FPA VAF Calculations

1. Evaluate Degree of Influence (DI) of each of the 14 GSCs mentioned below on a scale of 0 to 5.

2. Sum up the DIs of all 14 GSCs to arrive at total degree of influence (TDI)

   Maximum value of TDI = 70
   Minimum value of TDI = 0
   Typical value of TDI = 35

3. Calculate VAF as below,

   VAF = (TDI * 0.01) + 0.65
   Maximum value of VAF = 1.35
   Minimum value of VAF = 0.65
   Typical value of VAF = 1.00

18.2.5 Degree of Influence (DI) Calculations

- To be applied to each GSC
- Scale of 0 to 5
- General rule is as follows,
  0 - Not present or no influence
  1 - Incidental influence
  2 - Moderate influence
  3 - Average influence
  4 - Significant influence
  5 - Strong Influence

18.2.6 Fourteen General System Characteristics (GSC)

Sr. No	GSC
1	Data Communications
2	Distributed Processing
3	Performance
4	Heavily used configuration
5	Transaction rates
6	Online data entry
7	End user efficiency
8	Online update
9	Complex processing
10	Reusability
11	Installation ease
12	Operational ease
13	Multiple sites
14	Facilitate change

Assuming VAF = 1.0 and system developed in COBOL (20 hours/FP), time required will be,

(140 * 1) * 20 = 2800 Hours

18.3 Function Point Mark II

This is a further modification to *Function Point Analysis* method described earlier. This was developed by Charles Symons, Noolan, Norton & Co. UK based on the work carried out at Xerox, UK; this method is also called as *British Mark II – FPA*.

The changes from earlier method are, this method is driven by "functions", required "normalized" entities, need to know the accesses to entities, **high level design is required before counting**. This has high accuracy and less subjectivity as compared to FPA.

Five more new general system characteristics (GSCs) are added like interfaces, security considerations, direct access, documentation requirements and user training (please refer **Annexure - A**).

18.3.1 Steps of Function Point Mark II

Following steps are to be followed,

1. Decide the boundary of the system
2. List all "entities" with complete list of all data element types (DETs), a DET is a unique user recognizable field

---

3. List all "functions" performed by the systems
4. For each "function", count,

- DETs input to the function
- DETs output from the function
- Entities referenced by the function

5. Calculate unadjusted Mark II factor after applying weightages to input DETS, output DETS and entities referenced.
6. Calculate Mark II Value Adjustment Factor (MVAF)
7. Calculate Mark II Function Point Count (MFPC)

Entities: All user tables, system parameters treated as single entity, do not count files required for physical implementation, do not count files created for technical implementation.

Functions: These are as seen by the user e.g. create employee details, change of address, calculate monthly pay etc. Do not use functions used for technical implementation, do not count menu screens. A function must have at least one "input DET" and one "output DET" and one entity referenced. Do not consider backup, recovery etc.

Input DET is a unique user recognizable field that is required by the function as an input which may come from a screen or from an entity.

Output DET is a unique user recognizable field that is output by the function which may come on a screen or an entity or a report.

Do not count labels, legends, column headings, boxes etc. Count fields as the user views them e.g. employee details as one DET even though it may have more details.

Count all the entities referenced by the function. Entities may be referenced for add, modify, delete or read.

18.3.2 Mark II VAF Calculation

1. Evaluate Degree of Influence (DI) of each of the 19 GSCs on a scale of 0 to 5

2. Sum up the DIs of all 19 GSCs to arrive at total degree of influence (TDI)

   Maximum value of TDI = 95

   Minimum value of TDI = 0

   Typical value of TDI = 47.5

3. Calculate Mark II VAF as below,

   MVAF = (TDI * 0.005) + 0.65

   Maximum value of VAF = 1.125

   Minimum value of VAF = 0.65

   Typical value of VAF = 0.888

18.4 Class Complexity Based Approach

This method is for non MIS kind of systems, mainly systems developed using object oriented analysis and design (OOAD) approach and with graphical user interfaces and not character based systems.

1. Break the system into front end classes (GUI), Database or backend classes, Application classes and framework classes.

2. Apply complexity to these classes in terms of Simple, Medium, Complex and Very complex.

3. Use in-house metrix of Simple, Medium, Complex and Very Complex class timings for Coding and Unit Testing.

4. Apply overhead for Design, Testing, Project Management and Documentation.

The method has been designed and used by author in many non MIS kind of project.

For one of the organization in-house productivity to code Simple class, Medium class, Complex Class and Very complex class had been 3, 6,8,10 days respectively.

Simple method is one which involves plain assignment whereas complex method is a one which needs complex calculation.

Author categorized the classes as below,

Class Type	No. of simple methods per class	No. of complex methods per class	
Simple	3 to 5	0	
Medium	3 to 5	1 to 3	
Complex	5 to 8	3 to 5	
Very Complex	8 to 10	5 to 8	

Class Type	Number of Classes	Class coding and unit testing days	Total coding and unit testing days
Simple	10	3	30
Medium	6	6	36
Complex	4	8	32
Very Complex	2	10	20

Total coding and unit testing time = 118 person days

Other overhead 25% each, total time required will be 236 days.

Author found FPA not always suitable for OOA/OOD type of projects and/or GUI intensive and/or computational intensive, he designed the above simple method based on the data he gathered for many projects and arrived at class based estimation; it was very effectively used and found accurate. People can modify time required per type of class to code as per the productivity in their organization observed.

There are well published productivity for languages in FP book and also productivity for LOC per person per month depending on the size of projects, please see the chart below,

For productivity wherever each company should have its own matrix otherwise use it from FP handbook available on various web sites.

The class based method of estimation mentioned above can be used as per the context; FPA may not be recommended for GUI intensive projects but more suitable for MIS systems.

Also as per the stage of a system one should use either Mark I or Mark II if more details are known which are by and large known after the design. Mark I and II are recommended for MIS systems.

For Object Oriented projects we should use Class Complexity method.

We need to factor reusability in overall estimated efforts and calendar time.

18.5 Comparing the Size of Projects with Earlier Completed Similar Projects

Take into account complexity, try to normalize size of project to get how much efforts the new project will take. One can then relate new project similar to one of the earlier executed project and arrive at effort estimation approximately and in quick way.

18.6 Delphi Technique

Ask more than at-least two people to come out with their estimates independently and then arrive at final estimates. This helps to find any skew in the estimation.

Classify the projects as New Development, Enhancement, Porting, Migration etc.

For Enhancement, Porting, Migration projects ,it is worthwhile to do some quick pilot and arrive at final estimates e.g. how much time it will take to convert Forms from old version of Visual Basic to new version, do couple of forms conversion and then arrive at estimates.

One can use one or many of the followings parameters to arrive at size and using productivity norms we can estimate the efforts, these parameters can be,

1) LOC (Lines of Code) or SLOC (Source Lines of Code)
2) FP (Function Points)

3) Feature Points or Story Points in Agile
3) Number of Classes and their complexity
4) Number of Methods and their complexity

18.7 COCOMO (Constructive Cost Model)

This is a method to calculate person months, calendar months and relate person months of efforts to calendar months.

The method addresses three modes of software development, Organic mode, Embedded mode and Semi -detached mode.

The Calculation is based on Size in KLOC, Effect of Cost Drivers and Modes of Software development.

Organic Mode is a one where a small experienced team works in a familiar environment. The team members can communicate easily with each other and there are no stringent constraints. This is applicable for small to medium sized projects.

Embedded Mode is a one where large teams work. The team members cannot communicate easily with each other and there are stringent constraints. This is applicable for large sized projects.

Semi Detached Mode is a one between organic and embedded mode described above.

18.7.1 Basic COCOMO

Organic Mode

MM = 2.4 (KLOC)** 1.05
CM = 2.5 (MM)** 0.38

MM = Man months, CM = Calendar months

Embedded Mode

MM = 3.6 (KLOC)** 1.20
CM = 2.5 (MM)** 0.32

Semi Detached Mode

MM = 3.0 (KLOC)** 1.12
CM = 2.5 (MM)** 0.35

MM = Man Months, CM = Calendar months

18.7.2 Intermediate COCOMO

Organic Mode

MM = 3.2 *(CDM) * (KLOC)** 1.05
CM = 2.5 (MM)** 0.38

Embedded Mode

MM = 3.0*(CDM)* (KLOC)** 1.20
CM = 2.5 (MM)** 0.32

Semi Detached Mode

MM = 2.8*(CDM)* (KLOC)** 1.12

CM = 2.5 (MM)** 0.35

Where MM = Man Months and CM = Calendar Months

18.7.3 Cost Drivers

Where **CDM** (Cost Driver Multiplier) =
e1*e2*e3*.....*e15 as per the table below,

Attributes	Cost Drivers	Very Low	Low	Nominal	High	Very High	Extra High
Product	RELY	0.75	0.88	1.00	1.15	1.40	NA
	DATA	NA	0.94	1.00	1.08	1.16	NA
	CPLX	0.70	0.85	1.00	1.15	1.30	1.65
Computer	TIME	NA	NA	1.00	1.11	1.30	1.66
	STOR	NA	NA	1.00	1.06	1.21	1.56
	VIRT	NA	0.87	1.00	1.15	1.30	NA
	TURN	NA	0.87	1.00	1.07	1.15	NA
Personnel	ACAP	1.46	1.19	1.00	0.86	0.71	NA
	AEXP	1.29	1.13	1.00	0.91	0.82	NA
	PCAP	1.42	1.17	1.00	0.86	0.70	NA
	VEXP	1.21	1.10	1.00	0.90	NA	NA
	LEXP	1.14	1.07	1.00	0.95	NA	NA
Project	MODP	1.24	1.10	1.00	0.91	0.82	NA
	TOOL	1.24	1.10	1.00	0.91	0.82	NA
	SCED	1.23	1.08	1.00	1.04	1.10	NA

18.7.4 Cost Drivers Description

Cost Drivers	Description
RELY	Required software reliability
DATA	Data base size
CPLX	Product complexity
TIME	Execution time constraint
STOR	Main storage constraint
VIRT	Virtual machine volatility
TURN	Computer turnaround time
ACAP	Analyst capability
AEXP	Application experience
PCAP	Programmer capability
VEXP	Virtual machine experience
LEXP	Programming language experience
MODP	Modern programming practices
TOOL	Use of software tools
SCED	Schedule constraint

18.8 Detailed COCOMO

The detailed COCOMO is similar to intermediate COCOMO model except that project is divided into four phases: Product Design, Detailed Design, Coding/Unit Testing and Integration/Testing. The 15 cost drivers are calculated for each phase and applied separately instead of applying to whole project.

In the use of COCOMO for Calendar time estimation from MM (Man Months), we need to validate the COCOMO and rework coefficients used in COCOMO methods for each organization; this can be done from collected metrix in the organization.

18.9 Estimate Documents Contents

1) Total efforts in terms of person days
2) Calendar days
3) Sometimes range of effort estimates can also be specified when things are not very clear at initial stages of requirements

See sample below,

18.9.1 Efforts Estimates Contents

Sr.No.	Activity	Person Days
1	Requirements	
2	Architecture	
3	Detail design	
4	Coding	
5	Unit Testing	
6	System Testing	
7	Documentation	
8	Release Management	
9	Installation at client site	
10	User Acceptance	
11	Training to client	
12	Support post acceptance	
13	Project Management	
	Person Days	
	Person Months	

18.9.2 Work Schedule Details

Project Start Date :
Project End Date :
Team Size   :

Sr. No.	Activity	Person Days	No. of People	Elapsed Time (Weeks)	From Week	To Week
1	Requirement Study & Review					
2	Architecture & Review					
3	Design & Review					
4	Coding & Unit Testing					
5	System Testing					
6	Acceptance Testing					
7	Release					
8	Documentation					
9	Installation					
10	User Acceptance					
11	Training					
12	Support					
13	Project Management					

Total Elapsed Time will be around XX weeks i.e. around YY Months of elapsed time.

Total Efforts = NN Person Days (MM person months)

In the above schedule, there is no provision for contingencies which will arise, if any, during the course of the project.

This may take elapsed time from MM1 weeks to MM2 weeks.

18.10 Other Activity Durations to Be Factored in Estimation

While breaking the total efforts of a project take into account size of project (small, medium, big).

One can arrive at Coding and Unit Testing time and apply other overhead time like Design, Project Management, System Testing, and Documentation.

One should make provision for contingencies from 10% to 15% for small to big projects.

Use one day approximately, for 1000 lines of code reviewed by one person.

Time for internal review of software work products and software products by customer should be taken into account in overall efforts and elapsed time.

It is recommended to give range of efforts and range of calendar time when multiple estimates are arrived at.

18.11 Activity Estimates Based On Optimistic, Pessimistic and Most Likely Time

When an activity is to be estimated and following time exist,

a = most optimistic time,   b = most pessimistic time, m = most likely time

Then the activity time = (a+4m+b)/6 or
                   (0.25a+0.5m+0.25b)

The same formula can be used for overall efforts if we have three values for efforts.

18.12 Agile Estimations

Agile development focuses on various user stories form the backlog. Each user story is estimated by following different techniques.

18.12.1 Planning Poker

Estimation team has poker cards with values of 0, 1, 2,3,5,8,13,20,40 and 100. Product owner explain the requirement and each estimation team member assign a card, if all have the same values then it is accepted else card with maximum and minimum values and those who proposed them need to justify why they felt so to decide on final value.

18.12.2 T- Shirt Sizes

Just like S (small), M (medium), L (large), XL (extra-large), each estimation team member assign the size to each user story from the backlog and then with agreed value to Medium size of story, relative points are given to work out the estimates for all the user stories in a backlog.

18.13 Agile Project Plan

Here all Sprints are taken into account, each Sprint has multiple user stories, each story has been given priority, resources are allocated and start date and end dates, days allocated and status is captured.

Task Name	Person assigned	Start Date	End Date	Days	Status
Sprint 1					
Feature 1					
Features 2					
Sprint 2					
Feature 1					
Features 2					

18.14 Agile Release Plan

In Release plan all Sprints, their release dates are mentioned i.e. start date, end date, duration, status, release date and goals.

Sprint	Scope	Start Date	End Date	Duration	Status	Release Date	Goal
Sprint 1							
Sprint 2							
Sprint 3							

18.15 Velocity in Agile Development

It is a measure of amount of completed work in each Sprint by counting story points of all those stories done completely.

Stories which are not complete for whatever reasons are not considered.

This helps the team to complete remaining user stories in reasonable predictable time.

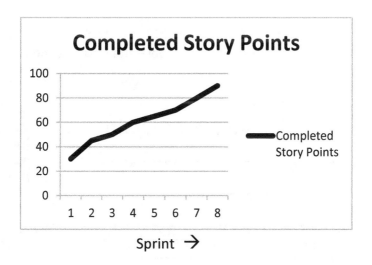

Figure 18.1 Velocity Chart

18.16 Burndown Chart in Agile Development

Burndown chart shows the team's progress in completing all the points they planned to complete in each Sprint. This is done after daily stand up meetings by Scrum Master.

Columns or Bars in Burndown chart shows the number of points of efforts remaining in the Sprint on day to day basis.

Sometimes new features get added or some defects get added to a story and may increase the efforts pending.

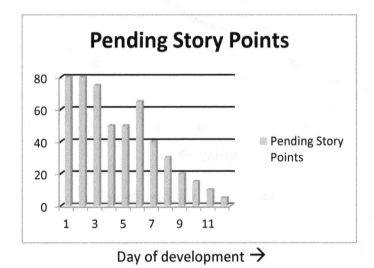

Day of development →

Figure 18.2 Burndown Chart

18.17 Risk in Estimation

Depending on the stage at which estimate is made, we should take into account the anticipated risk of we going wrong in estimation, please see the table below,

Stage when estimates were made	Actual estimate might be
Initial requirement definition	100 to 175%
Approved definition	90 to 150 %
Detail requirement analysis	70 to 120 %
Architecture	10 to 50%
Detail design	5 to 40%
Completion of product	2 to 20%

18.18 Good Practice in Estimation

Keep on re-estimating during the course of project at each phase of software development life cycle (SDLC) and apply feedback to keep project in control.

As you proceed from software requirement specifications to design to coding, testing, you have more clarity on the scope and more details about the system and hence estimation can be refined to manage the risks if any in terms of schedule.

Preserve old estimates and use as basis for future estimates by comparing similar projects or components.

Measure and monitor continuously throughout SDLC.

Collect the in-house metrix and productivity data to be used in the estimation and just don't go by published data, your own data will be more realistic and more useful.

Always estimate by more than one technique.

18.19 Distribution of Efforts per SDLC Stage

Given below are some approximate efforts per SDLC activity.

Activity	Approximate efforts of total project efforts
Requirement Analysis phase	5 – 10%
Architecture phase	5 – 10%
Design phase	10- 15%
Construction/Development	40 – 60%
Testing	15 – 25%
Release	5 – 10%
Documentation	5 – 8%
Project Management	10 – 15%

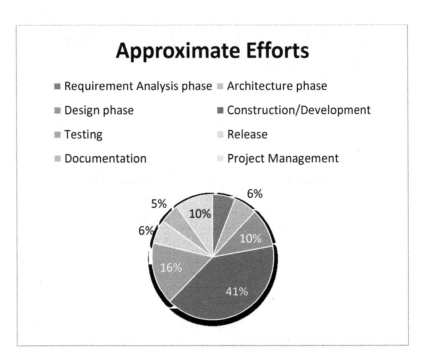

Figure 18.3 Approximate Efforts per SDLC Activity

18.20 Schedule Proportion of Activities in SDLC

Given below are some approximate percentages of overall schedule of elapsed time per SDLC activity.

Activity	Percentage of overall schedule of elapsed time of project approximately per SDLC activity
Requirement Analysis	5 - 10%
Architecture	10 - 15%

Design + Development + Testing	40 - 60%
Release	10 - 15%

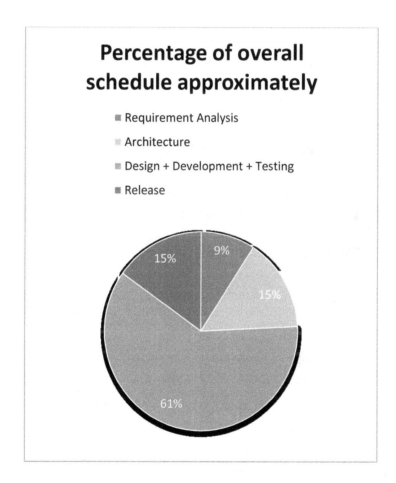

Figure 18.4 Percentage of Overall Schedule of Elapsed Time per SDLC Activity

Chapter 19

Project Failure

Big IT projects cost enormous and one never wants any project to be scrapped in the middle or not going live after it has been developed or it is not yielding required output and performance.

19.1 Reasons for Project Failures

There are many reasons why project fails and it is not always possible to pinpoint one reason for such failures.

The project may fail because of one or more of the following reasons,

1. Specifications were not clear and not frozen with client

2. Change management process not in place, requirements keeps on changing

3. Improper technology usage or unproven technology deployment

4. Client not taken into confidence so lack of ownership from client

5. Lack of ownership from management for one reason or another

6. Inadequate hardware while deployment

7. Unrealistic expectations of end client

8. Inadequate funding

9. Non profitable project for the development company

10. Incompetent development team, lack of skills

11. Lack of required tools

12. Lack of processes

13. Poor quality of deliverables consistently

14. Testing not up-to the mark to do proper test coverage

15. Consistent delays in committed milestone dates

16. Political opposition during implementation at client site

17. Resistance for change from client side and inability to adopt to routine style of operation

18. Failure in risk identification and mitigation leading to disaster

The above are some of the reasons why project fails.

If you see the above list you will notice that pure technical reasons or technology is less important factor towards project failures.

Its utmost important that all stakeholders of any project must be identified at the beginning and must be well catered to, their involvement and buying in is extremely important to make a project successful.

Chapter 20

Case Studies

20.1 Case Study 1

Client A was looking for an engineering software vendor.

Company's new sales office wanted to close first deal as early as possible.

The size of existing code was quite big and even to generate that existing code it took many years of efforts to the client in the past, whereas the actual re-engineered code became 4 times existing code with not much of reusability of client given earlier code, the efforts quoted were half of what it will take to develop, so actually efforts quoted were 1/8 of what would have required.

It had terrible impact on committed schedule, there were great efforts spent to achieve the target dates which were not practical and not possible.

At the end of first phase, client was highly disappointed and was explained the reality and downsizing of scope was done based on mutual discussions.

Learnings

- Never quote in hurry

- Be realistic

- Be transparent to customer

- Use scientific approaches in estimation for each category of projects i.e. new development, migration, maintenance etc.

- No use putting more resources to crunch the calendar time

- Better reduce the scope of project, prioritize the requirements and deliver them iteratively

20.2 Case Study 2

An overseas client wanted to develop a product.

Project manager was in touch with end client project manager. Earlier frozen requirement document was not strictly baselined. The requirements from end client kept on increasing and project manager kept on accommodating them in regular development.

The major change in technology from Java to VC/MFC was also made after the prototype was shown, as the speed was not so good with Java code. It was assumed that this change won't affect the efforts required but unfortunately it turned out to be different.

The client at one point start getting panic about the slippages and team started working hard to deliver in time, quality was affected.

The client was then explained the reality as matter got escalated and requirements were frozen at very late stage.

The product was developed but at the end client was unhappy for delay and never admitted that freezing the scope was critical and basic technology changes were harmful without doing proper impact analysis.

Learnings

- Freezing the specifications at the initial stages is very important
- Never make major technology changes without proper impact analysis
- Change management is very important
- Keep on reworking the impact of changes on efforts and schedule and keep client informed
- Ensure regular major milestone reviews with senior management to highlight scope changes and escalate issues before it's too late

20.3 Case Study 3

Client was complaining about code quality in one of his earlier project. It was decided that at the beginning of coding stage clear code review guidelines are adhered and also methodology of review.

The project had around 80 classes to be coded and a team of 5 developers were working during coding stage. They were told to write only 2 classes each and then sat for rigorous group code review. During the group code review 128 observations/defects were identified. Each team member made a note of it and all 128 observations were added to checklist.

Second group code review was decided after each member coded 5 classes and then again team assembled for group code review and third group code review was done at the end when each of the team members coded remaining assigned 10 classes.

During second group code review the observations decreased dramatically to a cumulative count of 10 and during last group code review the observations were almost zero.

The end code quality was superb.

Learnings

- Reviews are extremely important
- You can catch 70 to 80% defects in review
- Reviews needs to be planned properly
- Results of reviews needs to be shared to all concerned team members
- Sharing knowledge of others mistake is a great learning for others
- Foster team and group approach

20.4 Case Study 4

A web based system for HR department was developed for a client where information technology knowledge was very poor. No single person from client side was taking the ownership of the project and no one was committing the requirements towards freezing them.

The platform was also changed abruptly, starting with Access database with application running under NT to Windows 2000 server, SQL database. The issues of migrating data from excel to SQL were not thought properly.

The fear to reduce manpower due to computerization was always at the back of the minds of people in the client department. Systems acceptance was getting delayed and both parties were pointing towards each other.

Client side person giving requirements kept on changing throughout the project and each new person was describing what he wants rather than what the HR department wants.

The project manager was inexperienced and didn't intervene to stop the mess at early stage. Finally senior person had to intervene and he made sure that no new requirements will be addressed other than spelled earlier and one platform was fixed.

The data migration issues were first addressed and proper data was pulled in to new agreed SQL database.

System was completed and tested and delivered to client.

The client started using the system and came out with change request with list of new requirements as a separate project after proper consensus with their HR department, the second phase of project was smooth and took 33% of the time than earlier on proportionate scope basis.

Learnings

- Freeze the requirements first

- Ensure there is proper ownership from client side

- Involve the client and take their buying and commitment

- Freeze the platform, OS, Database etc. as target environment

- Never underestimate the importance of a good project manager and good project management practices

- Be tactful to address the lack of ownership issues or lack of IT knowledge at client side, if any

- Convince the client the benefits of the system like increase in productivity, ease of use, reduced mundane work etc., things will move fast, don't chase them too much ,let them chase you

20.5 Case Study 5

A client wanted to outsource the development work first time to an outside company. He approached two companies **A** and **B**. Both were told if the project was done in-house it will take 5 person years of efforts. Both **A** and **B** were asked to quote.

A went by clients efforts of 5 person years whereas **B** quoted almost 10 person years.

Client was impressed with **B**'s approach but decided to give contract to **A** as it was costing him almost half.

A started the development and client found things not being delivered as per commitment, the milestones were getting reached almost as per **B**'s schedule. **A** was panic; client was disappointed, as client has other product releases based on the outsourced project getting delivered in time.

Client has to delay all its end product releases, client lost substantial market due to delay in launching the product.

Client realized that **B** would have been better choice as the cost of project twice than that of **A** was far less than loss the client incurred due to loss of market share and reputation.

The detail analysis was done by client along with **B** and it was found that many important tasks like Specifications, Design, Testing, Project management gets no attention when a project is done in-house though a time is spent towards them but no one really keeps track of it except the development time, which was in this case just 50% of all project activities. **B** has highlighted this very clearly in their proposal.

Client learnt from **B** and decided to use **B** as best choice for its future projects.

Learnings

- Use scientific techniques for estimation
- Don't get convinced by anyone's efforts estimates unless you have done good homework
- Don't neglect tasks other than coding, you can't complete a project without them
- When you get skew in estimations, treat it as alarm and do proper analysis why the skew exist
- Share your development plans with client, be transparent

Chapter 21

Exercises

Below exercises are based on one new software system to be analysed, designed, architected and developed. These exercises will help to practice the concepts described in the various chapters of this book.

21.1 Software System to be developed

An automobile manufacturing company has thousands of parts going into the automobile to make a car. Some parts are manufactured in-house and some are purchased from external suppliers.

The production schedule which is based on the forecast of demand in the market, the number of cars to be produced will vary from week to week.

Company is looking for a software system to have just in time of supplied number parts from the vendors to have minimum inventory cost to maximise the profit.

The company has forecast software system used by sales and marketing departments and also production planning and scheduling system and inventory management system, but there is no centralised system which will interface with all these systems and act as an umbrella system to get real time data from all the other systems and also can input real time data to these other systems and should have centralised dashboard for the executive management to know the real-time status.

The system should be accessible from desktop as well as mobile devices and should be a web based system.

System must be fast, scalable, should have ease of use and secured.

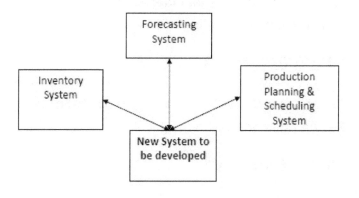

Figure 21.1 – New Software System to be developed

The existing three systems mentioned above are developed in Java, J2EE and have service oriented architecture.

User any standard source code control system, defect tracking system and other required tools for the various artefacts mentioned above in various exercises.

Based on this brief scope above, please work out the following exercises.

21.1.1 Exercise 1

Talk to the various stakeholders and create Business Requirement Document (BRD).

21.1.2 Exercise 2

Talk to the various stakeholders and create Functional Requirement Document (FRD).

21.1.3 Exercise 3

Talk to the various stakeholders and create Software Requirement Specifications (SRS).

21.1.4 Exercise 4

You have to assume that you need to develop two variants of system, one based on Structured System Analysis and Design (SSADM) and other based on OOAD.

Based on SSADM create the system analysis and design documents.

21.1.5 Exercise 5

Use Layered approach for the software architecture for the SSADM based system.

21.1.6 Exercise 6

Create object oriented analysis (OOA) and object oriented design document (OOD) for OOAD approach.

21.1.7 Exercise 7

Create UML diagrams for the OOAD approach development.

21.1.8 Exercise 8

Use Waterfall model for SSADM based development.

21.1.9 Exercise 9

Use Agile development for OOAD approach with Microservices architecture.

21.1.10 Exercise 10

Create Usability specifications, create wireframes and prototype.

21.1.11 Exercise 11

Create estimate documents for Waterfall approach along with schedule and optimum resource requirement using Function Point Analysis (FPA) method for SSADM approach based development.

21.1.12 Exercise 12

Create estimate documents for Waterfall approach along with schedule and optimum resource requirement using Function Point Mark II after the high level design is done for SSADM based system and compare with earlier estimates based on FPA.

21.1.13 Exercise 13

Create estimates for Agile based development using story points and work out different Sprints and schedule and resources.

21.1.14 Exercise 14

Create detail Project Plan.

21.1.15 Exercise 15

Create Configuration Management Plan.

21.1.16 Exercise 16

Create Risk Management Plan.

21.1.17 Exercise 17

Create Release Management Plan.

21.1.18 Exercise 18

Create Test Plans using V model of testing. Create test cases for unit testing, integration and system testing.

Chapter 22

Annexure – A

General System Characteristics (GSC)

(Reference: www.ifpug.org)

1. Data Communications

Score	Context
0	Pure batch or standalone PC
1	Batch with remote data entry or remote printing
2	Batch with remote data entry and remote printing
3	On-line data collection
4	On-line data update with remote data entry and remote printing
5	Supports multiple Tel-Processing protocols

2. Distributed Data Processing

Score	Context
0	Application does not aid the transfer of data or processing function between components of the system
1	Application prepares data for end user processing on another component of the systems such as PC spreadsheets and PC DBMS
2	Data is prepared for transfer, then is transferred and processed on another component of the system
3	Distributed processing and data transfer are on-line and in one direction only
4	Distributed processing and data transfer are on-line and in both directions
5	Processing functions are dynamically performed on the most appropriate component of the system

3. Performance

Score	Context
0	No special performance stated by the user
1	Performance and design requirements were stated but no special actions were required

2	Response time or throughput is crucial during peak hours. Feasibility can be established with minimal design effort
3	Response time is crucial during all business hours, Processing deadline requirements with interfacing systems are constraining
4	In addition, stated user performance requirements are stringent enough to require performance analysis benchmarking in the design phase
5	In addition, performance analysis tools are required in design, development and installation/ operational phases to monitor and tune performance

4. Heavily Used Configuration

Score	Context
0	No explicit or implicit restrictions are included (e.g. dedicated hardware).
1	Operational restrictions do exist, but are not very restrictive. No special effort is needed to meet restrictions.
2	Some security or timing considerations are required
3	Specific processor requirements for a specific piece of the application are included
4	Stated operation restrictions require special constraints on the application in the central processor

5	In addition, there are special constraints on the application in the distributed components of the system

5. Transaction Rate

Score	Context
0	No peak transaction period is anticipated
1	Monthly/ quarterly/ half-yearly/ annual peak transaction period anticipated
2	Weekly peak transaction period anticipated
3	Daily peak transaction period anticipated
4	High transaction rates stated by the user in the application requirements or service level agreements require performance analysis tasks in the design phase
5	High and unpredictable transaction rates stated by the user in the application requirements or service level agreements require performance analysis tasks and in addition, require the use of performance tools in the design, development and/or installation phases

6. On-line Data Entry

Score	Context
0	All transactions are processed in batch mode
1	1% to 7% of the transaction are interactive data entry
2	8% to 15% of the transaction are interactive data entry
3	16% to 23% of the transaction are interactive data entry
4	24% to 30% of the transaction are interactive data entry
5	More than 30% of the transactions are interactive data entry

7. End-User Efficiency

Following factors are to be considered,

- Navigational aids e.g. menus, function keys etc.
- Menus
- On-line help
- Automated cursor movement
- Scrolling
- Remote printing
- Pre-assigned function keys
- Batch jobs from on-line transactions
- Cursor selection of screen data
- Heavy use of highlighting
- Mouse interface
- Pop-up windows

- Optimized screen flow
- Multi-lingual support

End User Efficiency Factors

Score	Context
0	None of the factors are present
1	One to three of the above factors
2	Four to five factors
3	Six to eight factors are present
4	Nine or more factors present
5	In addition, end user efficiency is a strongly stated requirement

8. On-line Update

Score	Context
0	No on-line update
1	Some on-line update, volume is low, recovery is easy
2	Medium level of on-line update; volume is low; recovery is easy
3	High degree of on-line update
4	In addition, protection against data loss is essential and has to be specially designed and programmed
5	In addition, highly automated recovery procedures with minimal operator intervention are required

9. Complex Processing

Factors to be considered,

- Sensitive control and/or application specific security processing
- Extensive logical processing
- Extensive mathematical processing
- Much exception processing to handle incomplete transactions
- Complex processing to handle multiple input/ output possibilities, for example, multimedia or device independence

Score	Context
0	None of the factors are present
1	Any one of the above
2	Any two of the above
3	Any three of the above
4	Any four of the above
5	All five of the above

10. Reusability

Score	Context
0	Reusability is not a factor
1	Development to cater for the later enhancement within the application
2	Less than 10% code to be made reusable
3	10% to 20% code to be made reusable
4	20% to 35% code to be made reusable
5	Over 35% code to be made reusable

11. Installation Ease

Score	Context
0	No special considerations were stated by the user, and no special setup is required for installation
1	No special considerations were stated by the user, but special setup is required for installation
2	Installation requirements are stated by the user and installation guides are to be provided and tested. The importance of installation is not considered very important
3	Installation requirements are stated by the user. Installation guides are to be provided, Ease of installation perceived as very important by the user
4/ 5	In addition, tools are required to automate installation

12. Operational Ease

Score	Context
0	No special operational consideration other than normal back-up procedures were stated by the user
1/4	One, some or all of the following items apply to the application - Effective start-up, backup and recovery processes with significant operator intervention - Effective start-up, back-up and

	recovery processes with no operator intervention
	- In addition, application is to be designed for minimal operator intervention
5	Application is designed for unattended operation, Automatic error recovery is to be a part of the application

13. Multiple Sites

Score	Context
0	One user, single installation
1	Needs of multiple sites are to be considered in the design, to operate under identical hardware and software environments
2	Needs of multiple sites are to be considered in the design, to operate under similar hardware and software environments
3	Needs of multiple sites are to be considered in the design, to operate under different hardware and software environments
4	Documentation and support plan in addition to 2 above
5	Documentation and support plan in addition to 3 above

14. Facilitate Change

Score	Context
0	No flexible query/reporting
1	Flexible query and report facility using simple requests on single tables
2	Flexible query and report facilities using average complexity requests on multiple tables combined up to two
3	Flexible query and report facilities using complex requests on multiple tables combined
4	Flexible query and report facilities using simple. Average complexity requests with facility to save/reuse query
5	Flexible query and report facilities using complex requests with facility to save/reuse query

15. Requirements of Other Application

Score	Context
0	Systems is completely stand-alone
1 – 4	Requirement of the interface with few (1- 4) other applications
5	Requirement of interfaces with more than 4 other applications

16. Security, Privacy and Auditability

Score	Context
1	Personal privacy requirements
1	Special auditability requirements
2	Financial/ military
3	Require encryption of data

17. User Training Needs

Score	Context
0	No special user training material or courses to be prepared
1 – 4	Special training material e.g. on-line help, tutorial, training guide etc.
5	Special training simulation also required

18. Direct Use by Third Parties

Score	Context
0	No third party connection to the system
1	Data sent or received from third parties
2	Known third parties connected only for read mode
3 – 4	Known third parties connected directly with online update facilities
5	Unknown third parties can access the systems

19. Documentation Required

Score	Context
0	Up to 2 documents
1	3 – 4 documents
2	5 – 6 documents
3	7 – 8 documents
4	9 – 10 documents
5	More than 10 documents

Documents to be considered,

- Requirement specifications
- System Analysis
- System design
- Program specifications
- Test Plan
- User Manual
- Operation Manual
- Unit Test Packets
- System Test Packets
- Change Control
- Others

Glossary

A

APF	---- Adaptive Project Framework
API	---- Application Programing Interface
ATDD	---- Acceptance Test Driven Development

B

BaaS	---- Backend As A Service
BDD	---- Behavior Driven development
BRD	---- Business Requirement Document
BS	---- British Standard

C

CCPM	---- Critical Chain Project Management
CDM	---- Cost Driver Multiplier
CM	---- Configuration Management
CMP	---- Critical Path Method
CMU	---- Carnegie Melon University
COCOMO	---- Constructive Cost Model

D

DET	---- Data Element Type
DI	---- Degree Of Influence

E

ECM	---- Even Chain Methodology
EI	---- External Input
EIF	---- External Interface File
EO	---- External Output
EQ	--- -External Query

F

Faas	----	Function As A Service
FP	----	Function Point
FPA	----	Function Point Analysis
FPC	----	Function Point Count
FRD	----	Functional Requirement Document

G

GSCs	----	General System Characteristics
GUI	----	Graphical User Interface

H

HCI	----	Human Computer Interface

I

IEEE	----	Institute of Electrical and Electronics Engineers
ILF	----	Internal Logical File
ISO	----	International Standard Organization

L

L	----	Large
L1	----	First Line Support
L2	----	Second Line Support
L3	----	Third Line Support
L4	----	Product or Vendor Support
LOC	----	Lines Of Code

M

M	----	Medium
MFPC	----	Mark II Function Point Count
MM	----	Man Months
MVAF	----	Mark II Value Adjustment Factor

O

OOA	---- Object Oriented Analysis
OOAD	---- Object Oriented Analysis And Design
OOD	---- Object Oriented Design
OOM	---- Object Oriented Modeling
OS	---- Operating System

P

PMI	---- Project Management Institute
PMBOK	---- Project Management Book of Knowledge
PMP	---- Project Management Professional
PRINCE2	---- Projects IN Controlled Environments

Q

QA	---- Quality Assurance
QC	---- Quality Control
QE	---- Quality Engineering

R

RUP	---- Rational Unified Process

S

S	---- Small
SCCS	---- Source Control Configuration System
SDLC	---- Software Development Life Cycle
SEI	---- Software Engineering Institute
CMM	Capability Maturity Model
SLA	---- Service Level Agreement
SLOC	---- Source Lines Of Code
SRM	---- Software Release Management
SRS	---- Software Requirement Specifications
SSADM	---- Structured System Analysis and Design Method

T

TBD	----	Task Breakdown
TDD	----	Test driven development
TDI	----	Total Degree Of Influence
T & M	----	Time and Material Basis

U

UI	----	User Interface
UML	----	Unified Modeling Language
UPFC	----	Unadjusted Function Point Count
UX	----	User Experience

V

VAF	----	Value Adjustment Factor
VSS	----	Visual Source Safe

X

XL	----	Extra Large
XP	----	Extreme Programming
XPM	----	Extreme Project Management

Index

www.ingramcontent.com/pod-product-compliance
Lightning Source LLC
Chambersburg PA
CBHW071111050326
40690CB00008B/1184